ENGLiSH to 14

Liz Lockwood

Oxford University Press

ACKNOWLEDGEMENTS

The author and publisher are grateful for permission to reprint the following copyright material:

Nina Bawden: extracts from *Carrie's War* (Gollancz, 1973), Copyright © Nina Bawden 1973, reprinted by permission of Curtis Brown on behalf of Nina Bawden. **John Betjeman**: recipe for boiling an egg reproduced by permission of Desmond Elliott, Administator of the Estate of Sir John Betjeman. **Ray Bradbury**: extract from 'The Sound of Thunder' in *The Golden Apples of the Sun* (Rupert Hart-Davis), reprinted by permission of the Peters Fraser & Dunlop Group. **Yvonne Coppard**: extracts from *Everybody Else Does. Why Can't I?* (1992), reprinted by permission of the publishers, Piccadilly Press Ltd. **John Cotton**: 'In the Kitchen' from *Two by Two* by John Cotton and Fred Sedgwick (The James Daniel Daniel John Press, Ipswich), reprinted by permission of the author. **Roddy Doyle**: extract from *Paddy Clarke, Ha Ha Ha!* (Secker & Warburg, 1993), reprinted by permission of Reed Books. **Walter de la Mare**: 'Silver' from *The Complete Poems of Walter de la Mare* (1969), reprinted by permission of The Literary Trustees of Walter de la Mare, and The Society of Authors as their representative. **Eric Finney**: 'The Ice Dragons', first published in John Foster (ed); *Dragon Poems* (OUP, 1991), reprinted by permission of the author. **Anne Fine**: extract from *A Pack of Liars* (Hamish Hamilton Children's Books, 1988) Copyright © Anne Fine 1988, reprinted by permission of Penguin Books Ltd; extracts from *The Granny Project* (1986), reprinted by permission of the publishers, HarperCollins Publishers Limited. **William Golding**: extract from *Lord of the Flies*, reprinted by permission of Faber & Faber Ltd. **James Herriot**: extract from *Vet in a Spin* (Michael Joseph), reprinted by permission of David Higham Associates. **Susan Hill**: extract from *The Mist in the Mirror* (Sinclair Stevenson, 1992), reprinted by permission of Reed Books; extract from *I'm the King of the Castle* (Hamish Hamilton), Copyright © Susan Hill 1970, reprinted by permission of Richard Scott Simon Ltd. **Nigel Hinton**: extract from *Buddy* (J M Dent, 1982), reproduced by permission of the Orion Publishing Group Ltd. **Linda Hoy**: extract from *Your Friend Rebecca* (Bodley Head), reprinted by permission of Random House UK Ltd. **Jenny Joseph**: 'Warning' from *Selected Poems* (Bloodaxe Books Ltd), Copyright © Jenny Joseph 1992, reprinted by permission of John Johnson (Authors' Agent) Ltd. **Franz Kafka**: extract from *Metamorphosis*, translated by Willa & Edwin Muir (Secker & Warburg, 1948), reprinted by permission of Reed Books. **Laurie Lee**: lines from 'Christmas Landscape' in *Selected Poems* (Penguin), reprinted by permission of the Peters Fraser & Dunlop Group. **Ogden Nash**: 'The Wendigo', Copyright © 1952 by Ogden Nash, renewed, from *Verses from 1929 On* (Little, Brown and Company, 1959), reprinted by permission of Curtis Brown Ltd, New York. **Norman McCaig**: 'Frogs' from *Collected Poems* (Chatto & Windus), reprinted by permission of Random House UK Ltd. **Roger McGough**: lines from 'Snow and Ice Poems' in *Sky in the Pie* (Penguin Books, 1985), reprinted by permission of the Peters Fraser & Dunlop Group. **Mary O'Neill**: 'What is White' from *Hailstones and Halibut Bones* (Octopus), reprinted by permission of Reed Books. **Philippa Pearce**: extract from *Tom's Midnight Garden* (1958), reprinted by permission of the publishers, Oxford University Press. **Peter Porter**: 'Mort aux Chats' from *Collected Poems* (1983), reprinted by permission of the publishers, Oxford University Press. **Michael Rosen**: 'My Father's Father' from *When Did You Last Wash Your Feet?* (1986), reprinted by permission of the publishers, Scholastic Publications Ltd; first draft version reprinted by permission of the Peters Fraser & Dunlop Group Ltd. on behalf of the author. **May Swenson**: 'Was Worm' from *The Complete Poems to Solve* by May Swenson, Copyright © 1993 by The Literary Estate of May Swenson, reprinted by permission of Simon & Schuster Books for Young Readers, an imprint of Simon & Schuster Children's Publishing Division. **Rukshana Smith**: extract from 'blurb' for *Sumitra's Story*, (New Windmill), reprinted by permission of Reed Books. **J R Townsend**: extract from *Gumble's Yard* (Puffin Books), reprinted by permission of the author. **Paul Watkins**: extract from *Stand Before Your God*, reprinted by permission of the publishers, Faber & Faber Ltd. **Barbara Windsor**: extract from *Barbara, The Laughter and Tears of a Cockney Sparrow* (Hutchinson), reprinted by permission of Random House UK Ltd. **Robert Westall**: extract from *The Scarecrows* (Bodley Head, 1981), reprinted by permission of Random House UK Ltd; opening pages and front covers of *Blitzcat* (1989) and *The Promise* (1990), reproduced by permission of the publishers, Macmillan Children's Books.

Also for:

Clothes Show magazine cover, March 1996, copyright BBC Worldwide Limited 1996 (photograph by Nick Clements), reproduced by permission of BBC Worldwide Ltd. 'Clothes Show', the Clothes Show magazine logo, 'BBC' and the BBC logo are trade marks of the BBC.

Book reviews by Steve Rosson and Jonathan Weir from *Books for Keeps*, No 89, November 1994 (details of *BfK* can be obtained from 6 Brightfield Road, London SE12 8QF) reprinted by permission of Books for Keeps.

BT advertisement reprinted by permission of British Telecom.

Crown copyright maps from leaflet 'Runway Capacity to serve the South-East' - The Gatwick Option, local impact and wider impact, reproduced with the permission of the Controller of HMSO.

Chart from *The BMA Family Doctor Home Advisor* (1986), reproduced by permission of the publishers, Dorling Kindersley.

Front cover of Eurostar timetable and fares brochure reproduced by permission of European Passenger Services.

Extract from leaflet 'Hastings, Adventures in Time', text by Hastings Heritage Limited, illustrations by Brooker and How Limited, reproduced by permission of Hastings Borough Council.

Front cover of *New Musical Express*, 24.2.96, reproduced by permission of IPC Magazines, photograph reproduced with the permission of Steve Double.

Extract from Satellite TV listing from *What's On TV*, 2-8.3.96, reproduced by permission of IPC Magazines.

Extracts from *The Oxford School Shakespeare* and the *Oxford School Dictionary* (1994), reproduced by permission of Oxford University Press.

Grandprix 2 advertisement reprinted by permission of MicroProse.

The publisher would like to thank the following for permission to reproduce photographs: Tony Lees p.61 (bottom); Life File p.61 (top). Front cover photograph by Donald Cooper.

The illustrations are by: Roger Backwell pp.13, 21 (top), 33, 46; Simon Fell pp.19, 21 (bottom), 78, 96, 97; Rosamund Fowler pp.11, 124; Robert Goldsmith pp.49, 84, 88, 112; Michael Hingley pp.32, 38, 52, 80, 87, 111; John Holder p.120; Paul Hunt pp.66, 122; Tracy Newland pp.15, 29; Oxford Illustrators pp.7, 23, 94, 100, 116; Isabel Rayner p.35; Jon Riley pp.26, 75, 98, 106; Darrell Warner pp.45, 68, 103.

Handwriting and map on page 60 by Kathy Baxendale.

Although every effort has been made to trace and contact copyright holders before publication, we have not been successful in a few cases. If notified, the publisher will be pleased to rectify any errors or omissions at the earliest opportunity.

Introduction

English to 14 is aimed at students who are working towards the end of Key Stage 3. Each section focuses on a different area of language or literature, covering all the types of reading, writing, and talking that you are likely to meet, as well as giving you practice with some of the language and grammar points that you need to be aware of. You can use the book either in class, as directed by your teacher, or you can work with it on your own at home.

Section 1 focuses on language skills and grammar – the technical features of language. This covers areas you should be familiar with as well as areas that may be new to you, and the overall aim is to help you write accurately and show you how language works.

There is considerable emphasis in the National Curriculum on spoken English and Section 2 offers practical advice and plenty of opportunities for you to practise and develop your speaking and listening skills.

Reading for Information in Section 3 introduces you to some of the higher-order reading skills which are so important in the development of effective learning and study, and gives you practice with reading a wide variety of information texts.

Section 4 on Practical Writing has a twofold aim, giving you the chance of working with practical based units at the start then moving towards more creative work at the end.

The final two sections are wholly literature-based, and give guidance on how to read and respond to literature as well as practice on how to write about literature.

Learning about language and literature can be fun and I have tried to choose material that you will enjoy working with – some of it you will have met in class, while some will be new to you. I also hope that you will find it useful.

Liz Lockwood

Contents

SECTION 4: PRACTICAL WRITING

SECTION 5: READING LITERATURE

SECTION 6: WRITING ON LITERATURE

Nouns, Pronouns, and Adjectives

Objectives:

- to learn what nouns and pronouns are
- to understand what adjectives are and how they are used

What is a Noun?

A noun is the word class that is the name of something. It could be the name of a person, an object, a place, or an idea.

Collective nouns
groups of people, animals, or things:
e.g. flock, herd, band, bunch

Proper nouns
the names of particular persons, places or things, beginning with a capital letter:
e.g. Paris, Diana, January, Honda

Nouns

Common nouns
any person, place, or thing, but not one in particular:
e.g. sheep, car, person, place, month

Abstract nouns
the names of feelings or qualities that cannot be touched:
e.g. happiness, fun, love, hate

Activity See how many different kinds of noun you can find in the following limerick.

> A group of old fellows from Lyme
> They married three wives at one time.
> When asked, 'Why the third?'
> They replied, 'One's absurd,
> And bigamy, Sir, is a crime!'
> *Anon*

Pronouns and When They are Used

We use pronouns instead of nouns to avoid repeating the same nouns over and over again. Remember that you do have to mention the noun at least once so that everyone knows what you are talking about!

Personal pronouns
stand for people or things, without naming them:
e.g. I, you, he, she, it, we, they

Indefinite pronouns
do not stand for any definite noun, but are always linked with quantity:
e.g. every- some- no- any- + -one -body -thing

Pronouns

Possessive pronouns
show who owns something:
e.g. mine, yours (It is mine.)

Demonstrative pronouns
point out things:
e.g. this/these, that/those
(What is *that*? These are better than *those*.)

LANGUAGE SKILLS

Adjectives and Comparisons

Adjectives are the word class that add something to the meaning of nouns or pronouns. They help us to describe people, places, or things.

e.g. a *pretty* girl   a *crowded* shop   a *good* idea

They are also used when we compare two or more things with each other. These degrees of comparison are called:

- **positive** (for describing something on its own)
  e.g. a *thin* twig
- **comparative** (when two things are being compared)
  e.g. a *thinner* twig
- **superlative** (when more than two are being compared)
  e.g. the *thinnest* twig

(Remember: it is wrong to say 'the thinnest twig' when only two twigs are being compared.)

Most adjectives use comparison in this way, but we can also use the words 'more' and 'most'.

e.g. beautiful (positive)   *more* beautiful (comparative)
   most beautiful (superlative)

(Remember: we should not say 'more thinner' or 'most thinnest'. Use *-er* or 'more', *-est* or 'most'.)

Activity

Below is a very simple and dull opening to a story. Careful use of nouns, pronouns, and adjectives will transform it!

The (man) walked down the road. It was day. The man saw a house. The man walked up to the house and knocked on the door. The door opened and the man saw…

1 First of all find all the nouns. The first one has already been circled. Now rewrite the whole story by adding adjectives to describe these nouns, e.g. *The sad, limping man walked down the…*
   Note: some of the nouns may need to be changed to pronouns.
2 Try writing the basic story again, this time changing all the nouns and adding adjectives to create a Science Fiction or Horror Story opening.
3 Now change all the nouns and add a variety of adjectives to make the same basic story sound like a Nursery Rhyme or Fairy Tale.

Follow-up
- For more practice using nouns and adjectives, see page 10.
- For more on imaginative writing, see pages 76–77.

Verbs

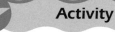

- to understand what verbs are
- to understand what tenses are and when they are used

What is a Verb?

Verbs are the word class that gives us information about what is happening in a sentence:

- the *action* someone or something is performing: e.g. kick, dance, skip
- the *state* s/he or it is in: e.g. appear, feel, seem
- the *process of change* s/he or it is going through: e.g. turn, grow, become

Activity

The same basic story from the Activity on page 7 is repeated below. This time change all the verbs, which have been highlighted for you. Try to choose new verbs that emphasize that the man is frightened and in a hurry. You can also add adjectives and change the nouns if you want to.

> The man walked down the road. It was day. The man saw a house. The man walked up to the house and knocked on the door. The door opened and the man saw…

Tenses

Any action that happens must happen at a certain time. The term tense is used when we want to refer to this.

> Today, Sunday, I am having a rest. (*present* tense)
> Last night I went to a disco. (*past* tense)
> Tomorrow I will go to school again. (*future* tense)

> **Instructions to a Spy!**
>
> On Monday night you will catch the 8.00 p.m. train to Bolton. The person you will be following will also be on that train. You will be able to identify him by the distinctive hat that he will be wearing and by the fact that he will be walking with a limp. You will keep him within your sight at all times.
>
> When you reach Bolton, you will follow him to his home and wait there, out of sight, for further instructions.

Activity

The above instructions have been written in the future tense. Imagine that you have carried out this mission. Write your diary entry for what actually happened. This will need to be in the past tense. Make it as vivid and realistic as you can and aim for 200–300 words. It might start something like this:

> It was hard to believe how my mission last Monday turned out. I was instructed to catch the 8.00 p.m. train to Bolton. It was a cold, wet, and windy night…

Verbs can appear in different forms as well as in different tenses.

Infinitive

The base form of the verb (with no endings) is often known as the infinitive: e.g. to run, to hit, to sing.

I try very hard *to hit* the ball when I play tennis!

Past participle

The *-ed* form, made by adding *-ed* to the base, is often known as the past participle: e.g. kicked, danced, rented.

A really pretty villa was *rented* for our holiday in Spain last year.

Present participle

The *-ing* form, made by adding *-ing* to the base, is often known as the present participle: e.g. visiting, kicking, dancing.

I love danc*ing* when I go to discos or parties.

Auxiliary Verbs

Sometimes we need auxilary verbs. These are additional verbs that tell us more about the main verb:

* *when* it is happening (she *will* be going to school)
* if it *ought* to happen (she *ought* to go to school)
* if it *has* to happen (she *must* go to school)

Here are the main auxiliary verbs you are likely to come across:

will	shall	would	should	
do	does	did	done	doing
may	might	must	ought to	
be	am	is	are	was
were	being	been	can	could
has	have	had	having	

Many auxiliary verbs get shortened and we use apostrophes to fill the gap of the missing letters:

She <u>should have</u> gone to school becomes she <u>should've</u> gone to school.

Working on

You are going to write a short poem of seven lines in the shape of a diamond, using only nouns, adjectives, and verbs. It is called a diamante. First you need to think of two nouns that are opposites, e.g. heat, cold.

heat
unbearable, relentless
scorching, frying, baking
swimsuit, sunhat, gloves, scarf
freezing, biting, shivering
extreme, deadly
cold

Line 1 – The 1st noun
Line 2 – 2 adjectives connected with the 1st noun
Line 3 – 3 verbs (present participles) connected with the 1st noun
Line 4 – 4 nouns moving from the 1st to the 2nd noun
Line 5 – 3 verbs (present participles) connected with the 2nd noun
Line 6 – 2 adjectives connected with the 2nd noun
Line 7 – The 2nd noun

Now think of some opposites and write a diamante using this model.

Follow-up

* For help on nouns and adjectives, see pages 6–7.
* To learn more about poetry writing, see pages 82–83.

Adverbs, Prepositions, Conjunction

What is an Adverb?

Adverbs are parts of speech that tell us more about verbs, adjectives, or other adverbs. While verbs tell us what is happening, adverbs tell us:
• how something is happening (adverbs of *manner*)
  e.g. boldly, neatly, cheerfully, madly, etc.
• when it is happening (adverbs of *time*)
  e.g. often, early, tomorrow, weekly, etc.
• where it is happening (adverbs of *place*)
  e.g. under, below, here, there, etc.
• to what degree it is happening (adverbs of *degree*)
  e.g. nearly, quite, too, very, etc.

Activity

Using the same outline story from the previous section (printed below), add adverbs where there are gaps. Try to choose adverbs that emphasize that the man is frightened and in a hurry. You can add adjectives and change the nouns and verbs if you want to.

The man walked .... down the road.

It was .... day. The man .... saw a house.

The man walked .... up to the house and knocked

.... on the door. The door opened .... and the

man .... saw ...

Working on

You could also try experimenting with the different parts of speech by making up nonsense poems.

1 Choose a topic (e.g. Autumn) and list six adjectives. Then list six nouns, six verbs, and six adverbs in columns:

Adjectives	Nouns	Verbs	Adverbs
golden	leaves	flutter	gracefully
smoky			
busy			
red			
mellow			
sleepy			

2 Then either choose at random or throw a dice to decide which words will go together. They must always be in the order adjective, noun, verb, adverb.
3 Write your results down as a poem. When you have completed your poem, try to assess how well each line works and make any changes you think are necessary.
4 Choose a different topic and start again.

What is a Preposition?

A preposition is a word which is always followed by a noun or pronoun and together these tell us where or how something happens.

e.g. The boat sails *under* the bridge.

Here are some common prepositions:

about above across after along among around at
before behind below beneath beside between by
down during except for from in inside into near
of off on onto out over round since
through to towards under until up with

Activity

Choose a topic (e.g. a tree) and write six lines about it, each one beginning with or containing a different preposition. Here is an example:

Under the tree lie drifts *of* golden leaves.
Inside the tree the sap slowly sinks.
Beside the tree a squirrel scrabbles *for* acorns.
Above and *beyond* the tree migrating birds swirl past.
Around the tree the last meadow flowers die away.
Behind the tree the autumn sun glows golden red.

Now try and write your own preposition poem on any topic of your choice. You do not have to start each line with a preposition, as above, but use the example as a guide if it helps.

What is a Conjunction?

A conjunction is a word that joins other words and groups of words together. Here are some common conjunctions:

and but or so either neither nor although before
if after that unless when while until since because

Rather than writing several simple sentences, it is often better to join them with conjunctions. This varies the pace of the writing for the reader. For example instead of saying:

It rained all day. We had to stay indoors.

you could say either of the following two sentences:

It rained all day, *so* we had to stay indoors.
As it rained all day, we had to stay indoors.

(Notice that a comma is used where the original first sentence ended.)

What is an Interjection?

An interjection usually expresses some sort of emotion or feeling (approval, concern, relief, surprise, annoyance, etc.). You will see that it is often followed by an exclamation mark. Here are some examples:

Hello! Good gracious! Oh dear! Shhh! Hm! Ugh! Ow!

Follow-up

- To learn more about different types of sentence, see the following unit.
- To learn more about poetry writing, see pages 82–83.

Sentences and Phrases

What is a Sentence?

It is not as easy as you might think to say exactly what a sentence is. In writing, a sentence:

- begins with a capital letter and ends with a full stop, question mark, or exclamation mark
- is a group of words usually put together according to grammatical rules (see 'Subjects and predicates' below)
- can be spoken or written on its own without the feeling that it is incomplete

Types of sentence

There are three main types of sentence that you will come across:

- **a statement**: James likes dogs.
- **a question**:   Do you like dogs?
- **a command**: Go home, Fido!

Subjects and predicates

Every sentence usually has a subject and a predicate.

- The **subject** is what the sentence is about and is usually a noun or a pronoun. Subjects often come at the beginning of sentences.
- The **predicate** is the rest of the sentence. It tells what the subject is doing or what happens to the subject. The predicate contains a verb.

subject	predicate	
James	likes dogs.	(statement)
Who	likes dogs?	(question)
Fido	go home!	(command)

The subject does not always come at the beginning of the sentence:
  e.g. After the crash came a noise of breaking glass.
To find the subject you must:

- pick out the main verb (came)
- ask yourself What? or Who? (What came? or Who came?)

The answer to the question will be the subject of the sentence (a noise of breaking glass).

Simple sentences

A simple sentence has only one subject and one predicate.

  My name is Elizabeth.
  I was born in London.

If you use too many simple sentences in your writing, it sounds rather abrupt and becomes monotonous.

  I am fourteen years old. I like animals. I have a pet rabbit.
  I have a pet cat. I have two goldfish. I would like a dog.
  My mum will not let me have a dog.

Co-ordinated sentences

Using conjunctions to form co-ordinated sentences is one way to vary your writing and make it more interesting. A co-ordinated, or compound sentence consists of two or more simple sentences joined by the conjunctions 'or', 'and', or 'but'.

My name is Elizabeth, *and* I was born in London.

Activity

Look at the seven simple sentences about pets at the bottom of page 12. Using conjunctions, make them into several co-ordinated sentences.

Phrases

Phrases are groups of words that make sense but are incomplete.
They may be lacking a subject, or they may be lacking a predicate:

in the sun (no subject)   her new shoes (no predicate)

They can also do the work of nouns in a sentence:

The *road* was quiet. (noun)

The road, *an avenue of newly planted trees*, was quiet. (noun phrase)

or the work of adjectives:

The *brown-eyed* child was crying. (adjective)

The child *with brown eyes* was crying. (adjectival phrase)

or adverbs:

Lucy went out *silently*. (adverb)

Lucy went out *without making a sound*. (adverbial phrase)

Some groups of words are not phrases because they don't make any sense:

being rabbit she light leg sing

Activity

Look at the phrases below and try to expand them into sentences to make a complete short story. You will need to add subjects to some of the phrases and predicates to others.

in the car   on a mountain   terrible conditions   too fast
sharp bend   terrible crash

Follow-up
- For more help on nouns and pronouns, see page 6.
- For more help on verbs, see pages 8–9.
- For more help on conjunctions, see page 11.

Clauses and Complex Sentences

What is a Clause?

A clause is a group of words which forms part of a sentence but which has a subject and predicate of its own. This makes it different from a phrase, which often does not have either a subject or a predicate.

    sentence: It started to rain when he went for a walk.
    phrase: for a walk
    clause: when he went for a walk

There are several different types of clause.

Noun clauses

These do the work of nouns or noun phrases.

    The *road* was quiet. (noun)
    The road, *an avenue of newly planted trees*, was quiet. (noun phrase)
    It is delightful *that the road is so quiet*. (noun clause)

Adjectival clauses

These do the work of adjectives or adjectival phrases.

    The *brown-eyed* child was crying. (adjective)
    The child *with brown eyes* was crying. (adjectival phrase)
    The child, *who had brown eyes*, was crying. (adjectival clause)

Adverbial clauses

These do the work of adverbs or adverbial phrases.

    Lucy went out *silently*. (adverb)
    Lucy went out *without a sound*. (adverbial phrase)
    When Lucy went out, she did not make a sound.
    (adverbial clause)

Notice that all the clauses contain main verbs. Can you pick them out?

Main clauses and subordinate clauses

- When a clause forms the main statement in a sentence, it is called a *main clause*.
- When a clause does the work of nouns, adjectives, or adverbs (see above), it depends on the main clause for its meaning. It is called a *subordinate clause*.

For example, in the following sentence:

    When I am hungry, I eat too many biscuits.

the clause 'I eat too many biscuits' can stand by itself and make sense, so it is a main clause. 'When I am hungry' does not make complete sense on its own. It depends on the main clause to complete its meaning, so it is a subordinate clause.

Understanding how to use these different ways of expressing yourself should help you:

- become more aware of your own style of writing
- make your writing more varied and interesting

The last unit ('Sentences and Phrases') suggested you should avoid using too many simple sentences. Using co-ordinated sentences is one way of adding variety to your writing. Another way is to experiment with complex sentences or a mixture of the two – co-ordinated complex sentences.

What is a Complex Sentence?

A complex sentence is one which contains one main clause and one or more subordinate clauses. It also uses the full range of conjunctions available, unlike a co-ordinated sentence.

e.g. When I am hungry, I eat too many biscuits.

What is a Co-ordinated Complex Sentence?

A co-ordinated-complex sentence is one which contains two or more main clauses and one or more subordinate clauses.

e.g. When the shop opened, he went in and started to look for some new clothes.

Activity

1 Read the following passage which has been written mostly in simple sentences.

John went shopping. He bought a newspaper at the newsagents. Then he went to the supermarket. He bought some bread and some butter. Then he chose some chicken and chips. These were for his evening meal. He thought he would also like something sweet. He could not decide what to choose. He thought about a fruit pie. He also wondered about some fresh fruit. He was very undecided. He chose some strawberries. That was everything. He went home.

2 Rewrite the passage using only a mixture of simple and co-ordinated sentences.

3 Write it again adding complex and co-ordinated complex sentences.

4 Write a paragraph of your own about your family or the way you come to school. Concentrate on making your writing interesting by varying your sentence structure.

Follow-up
- For more help on subjects and predicates, see page 12.
- For more help on nouns and adjectives, see pages 6–7.
- For more help on adverbs, see page 10.
- For more help on simple and co-ordinated sentences, see pages 12–13.

Punctuation: Basic Revision

Why Do We Use Punctuation?

When people are talking, they repeat themselves, hesitate, pause, and use gestures to break up their sentences and make their meanings clear. Written words are very different and have to rely on punctuation and grammar for their meanings. Punctuation keeps writing under control and tells readers when to pause, when to hesitate, and who is doing what.

Capital Letters and Full Stops

Capital letters and full stops help us to work out what is going on. Capital letters should be used for:

• the first letter of every sentence: **W**e always let our rabbit hop round the garden.
• the word 'I': When we go out in the car, **I** like to sit in the back.
• the first letter of proper nouns: **L**ucy, **V**ictoria, **T**hursday, **L**ondon
• initials and abbreviations: **C. S.** Lewis, **BBC**
• the main words in titles: Under the **G**reenwood **T**ree
• the first word in direct speech: She asked, '**C**an we go too?'

Full stops should be used:

• to end a sentence: We always let our rabbit hop round the garden**.**
• after initials: C. S. Lewis
• after some abbreviations: Bucks**.** (short for Buckinghamshire)

Note: Questions normally end with a question mark: e.g. Do you like this? Exclamations normally end with an exclamation mark: e.g. Listen to me! (You don't need a full stop as well as a question mark or an exclamation mark.)

Commas

Commas are used to help readers understand what is being said or written in a sentence. They divide parts of a sentence to make meanings clearer. Commas should be used:

• to separate words in a list
    e.g. The rabbit was hot, bothered, cross, and exhausted.
• to separate the clauses in a sentence
    e.g. Whenever he saw the cat, he chased her.
• to mark off phrases in a sentence
    e.g. The cat, thoroughly fed up, slept all day.
• to mark off individual words and connectives
    e.g. However, no real harm was done.
• in direct speech
    e.g. Victoria came in and asked, 'Whatever has happened?'

Activity

1 Write out the following sentence opener, and complete the sentence with six listed items.

> I went shopping to buy …

2 Write out the following sentences, adding commas where appropriate.

> My gran wins when we play cards but I can beat her at darts.
> Tom the man next door said he had heard all the noise.
> Michael come and wash your hands.
> The teacher said 'Do this work on your own.'

Apostrophes

Apostrophes seem to cause a great deal of trouble, and many people use them in the wrong places.

Apostrophes should be used to show:

- where letters have been missed out:

> 'Let's (let us) go out into the garden. We're (we are) too hot to stay indoors. You're (you are) looking so pale, I'll (I will) go and get Mum. In fact I think I should've (should have) called her sooner.'

- that something belongs to somebody:

  If there is only one owner, you add -'s:

> Please give me the teacher's books. (the books belonging to a teacher)

  If there is more than one owner, you add -' onto a plural ending in -s:

> Please give me the teachers' books. (the books belonging to the teachers)

  When the plural does not end in -s, you need to add -'s:

> The men's boots were dirty. (the boots belonging to the men)

Note: you don't need to use an apostrophe with possessive pronouns, e.g. yours, ours, theirs, its, his, hers. Also, it's with an apostrophe means it is. The apostrophe is to show that the i has been missed out of the word is, not to show that anything belongs to it.

Activity

There are six apostrophes in the two sentences below.

> I'd like to go to James's party if you're going too, Dean.
> Jodie said she'd bring some of her brother's CDs, which should be a bit better than those girls' tapes!

1 Draw a chart of two columns headed:

Apostrophes to show missing letters   Apostrophes to show possession

List the words and phrases using apostrophes in the appropriate column and then write out what they mean in full, without their apostrophe. Add more examples of your own in each column.

2 Write out your own series of sentences as a paragraph or short story. Use apostrophes to show missing letters and to show ownership. Write your paragraph in the present tense and include some direct speech.

Follow-up

- For help on tenses, see page 8.
- To check how to punctuate direct speech, see page 80.

Inverted Commas and Colons

Inverted Commas

In direct speech

Inverted commas, or quotation marks, are most commonly used to punctuate direct speech. The rules for doing this can be found on page 80. If you cannot remember them, you should revise them now.

Looking at the following words, which have no punctuation, we cannot tell if the man has stumbled or the girl has stumbled:

the man said the girl had stumbled

They can be punctuated in two different ways:

• as a **statement**: The man said the girl had stumbled.
• as a piece of **direct speech**: 'The man,' said the girl, 'had stumbled.'

For quotations within quotations

When you are quoting what someone else wrote or said within existing quotation marks, you should use double quotation marks:

'You know what your mum will say when she finds out, don't you?' said Jill. 'She'll say, "If I catch you doing that again, you'll be grounded for a week!", so I think we'd better not go.'

For titles

Titles of films, television and radio programmes, plays, books, and poems are usually shown within single quotation marks:

I wasn't allowed to go and see 'Frankenstein'.

Activity

1 Look carefully again at the two sentences showing quotations within quotations (reprinted below). Take each item of punctuation in turn and try to explain in writing why that particular punctuation mark has been used. There are 21 punctuation marks to write about.

'You know what your mum will say when she finds out, don't you?' said Jill. 'She'll say, "If I catch you doing that again, you'll be grounded for a week!", so I think we'd better not go. We can always see 'Frankenstein' another time.'

2 Write out a dialogue between a shop assistant and a customer who is trying to return some faulty goods. Use direct speech, and as many other punctuation marks as you think you should practise.

Colons and Semicolons

A colon looks like this : and is usually used:

• to show that some sort of a list will follow:

All sorts of famous people were there: film stars, Members of Parliament, television celebrities, and even Royalty.

• to introduce a saying or a statement:

I'm often late for school: getting up early is impossible!

• to introduce direct speech if there is a long lead up to it

A semicolon looks like this **;** and is usually used:

- to separate lengthy items in a list
- between two clauses to show a pause that is longer than a comma, but shorter than a full stop:

> The abandoned puppies were a sorrowful sight: one was whimpering softly; another was too weak even for that; a third was lying limply against its brother; all three were cold, bedraggled, and wet.

- to join two sentences which are close in thought and of equal weight to make a longer sentence. The semicolon balances them:

> The winter has been very cold this year; the snow has been falling for days.

Activity   Try to punctuate the following passage by copying the story out and marking in the pauses as you go along. Before you do any writing, read the passage out loud, trying to work out where these pauses should be. Then decide whether they should be marked by commas, full stops, colons, or semicolons. Add capital letters where appropriate as well.

The Kidnapping

we didn't know whether to trust them or not our train was due to arrive at four o clock we were due at the house by five we had been given these instructions take the number 18 bus from the station look for your next instructions on the back seat upstairs inside a copy of the mirror cracked from side to side we found that all right and the address inside it the only problem was that the address was difficult to read it had been put together by cutting out letters from a newspaper perhaps they were making sure their handwriting wouldn't be recognized a handwriting expert certainly wouldn't get far with that we didn't think there'd be any fingerprints either the kidnappers weren't likely to make that sort of mistake still although the address was hard to read our instructions were clear on arriving at the house go straight to the telephone box opposite number six wait for a call we were told Carlos would ring at 5.05 and if we didn't answer Andrew the best detective in the south would be killed with our hearts pounding we approached the telephone box just as it began to ring I stretched out my hand to lift the receiver when a loud voice bellowed 'stop this is the police' it seemed we were surrounded there were suddenly torches sirens blue lights cars and people everywhere my heart sank I felt weak at the knees what was going to become of Andrew now?

Follow-up
- For more practice punctuating direct speech, see page 41.
- For more help on capital letters, full stops, and commas, see pages 16–17.

Paragraphing

Objectives:

- to understand what paragraphs are and why we use them
- to be able to group linked ideas together
- to be able to develop a sequence of paragraphs

Why Do We Use Paragraphs?

The main reason for having paragraphs is to give the reader a rest! If we did not divide our writing up into sections, then it would be very difficult to follow and understand. Every time we end one paragraph and start a new one we are saying, 'Did you understand that point? Then I'll go on to the next.' A new paragraph also shows a change of speaker in dialogue.

What are Paragraphs?

All the information in any one paragraph should be concerned with the same aspect of a subject – basically, paragraphs are units of thought. Often in each paragraph there is one particular sentence, the topic sentence, which tells the reader what that paragraph is about. Every sentence in the paragraph should be connected with that idea in some way.

You should always start a new line for each new paragraph. If you are writing by hand, start writing about two centimetres from the margin of your page. This is called indenting.

In the following short paragraph, it is easy to see which is the topic sentence and which sentence is out of place.

Dogs

Dogs make very good pets. They are usually very affectionate to their owners and respond well to good treatment. As companions, they are second to none and are universally known as 'Man's best friends'. Cars are very noisy.

Find the topic sentence in the following paragraph.

Early Memories of School

Our teachers were feared rather than liked. They all seemed to be fierce old ladies. There was no talking in class unless we were spoken to. There was smacking and, later, caning for those who were deemed to have misbehaved. Those who had not learned their lessons properly ran the risk of being stood in the corner, in front of the class, face to the wall with the dunce's cap on. (This was a sort of pointed conical affair with a big 'D' on it.) A group punishment I particularly disliked was when we had to sit with our hands on our heads, fingers interlocked, for what seemed like eternity. Discipline was strict.

Activity

Sequencing ideas is important. Just as individual paragraphs need to hold together as individual units, in a longer piece of writing, paragraphs also need to follow on from each other in a logical order, so the piece of writing makes sense.

1 Put the following pictures into the right order and then write a six-step (six-paragraph) description of what is happening in the story. Aim to make each paragraph at least four or five sentences long.

Leaving the shop

Going into town

Buying a shirt

Window shopping

Showing off the new shirt

Trying a shirt on

Have you seen this person?

2 Practise writing your own paragraphs, each with a topic sentence, in a logical sequence. Imagine *Crimewatch* is trying to trace a particular person. You need to supply the written details needed to build up an identikit picture.

First paragraph This should contain information about the person's appearance: name, age, build, hair colour, facial details.

Second paragraph This should develop descriptions of the sort of clothes the person was last seen wearing: what sort of style and fashion, what colours, what sort of shoes.

Third paragraph Here you could describe the characteristics and habits the person has: mannerisms, styles of talking, walking.

Fourth paragraph Finish by describing the person's general attitude.

Concluding paragraph What is your overall opinion of this person?

Follow-up
- For more practice writing accurate descriptions, see pages 70–71.
- For more practice concentrating on character, see pages 90–91.

Word Origins

Historical Roots

Many words in our language have their origins in other languages – from the past and the present.

Old English			Middle English		Modern English
Romans in Britain – Latin used by the Church until 1500s	**Angles and Saxons invade**	**Vikings invade**	**1066 Norman Conquest – French used at Court**	**Scholars use many Latin and Greek words**	**Trade, travel, exploration, and inventions all bring new words**
nun	cow	kid	tax	debt	tea
hymn	hen	sky	pork	doubt	vodka
candle	axe	skull	beef	island	gorilla
captain	sail	skill	court	ache	guinea
fountain	crop	dike	prison	scissor	totem
education	farm	wing	castle	receipt	steppe
society	field	outlaw	prince	pauper	tycoon
benefit	arrow	crooked	wages	index	kowtow
priest	goose	ugly	money		outback
abbot	sheep		baron		moccasin
angel	plough		justice		kangaroo
			mutton		balalaika
			royalty		

English Language

Borrowed Words

There are many other words from many other languages that have been borrowed and adapted:
- **Indian**: cushy, polo, pal, pukka, dungarees, bungalow, chutney, yoga, pepper, ginger, loot, bangle, shampoo, pyjamas, curry, dinghy, panda, cheetah, catamaran
- **Celtic**: tweed, jag, rub, haggis, crag, clan, caber, button, badger, glen, jockey, coracle, galore, leprechaun, shamrock, whiskey, kilt, bog, job, druid
- **Dutch**: scone, uproar, spool, deck, loiter, landscape, nitwit, hiccup, groove, hobble, hoist, bury, skipper, hope, knapsack, boss, dock, splint, luck, wagon
- **Italian**: pilgrim, dentist, corridor, stiletto, piano, studio, traffic, carnival, volcano, arcade, opera, confetti, concert, spaghetti, umbrella, macaroni, accelerate, buffoon, inferno, balcony

Activity Choose one of the groups of borrowed words on page 22 and write a short story or description using as many of its words as you can. You will need to choose a subject and tone that is appropriate to your chosen vocabulary.

The Continual Process of Change

English changes in other ways too. Once a word is part of a language, it doesn't necessarily keep the same meaning forever. Sometimes meanings of words change completely and sometimes words and meanings pass out of use and vanish altogether.

Activity

1 Study the changes in meaning that have happened to the word 'nice' (see below) and try to explain why you think the meaning of the word has undergone each change. You may need to make some guesses! Its original root was the Latin word *nescius*.

Latin: *nescius* = ignorant, inattentive

1350 foolish, stupid

1600 lazy, slothful

1700 difficult to please,
fussy about small things

1800 carefully accurate

Now pleasant

2 Carry out some similar research on one or more of the following words: silly, sensible, gossip, handicap.

Working on

1 Changes and borrowings take place all the time in a wide variety of areas. Here are some new words. Can you think of any others?

Commerce capital, discount, insurance, budget
Politics cabinet, democrat, liberal, Prime Minister
Art Forms Impressionism, Cubism, Surrealism
Music jazz, rock, pop, backing
Space blast-off, satellite, astronaut, module
War Blighty, blitz, holocaust, scud

2 Words linked with fashion and items of clothing are constantly changing. Do you know what the following items of clothing are? Use a dictionary to find out what they mean, then try drawing and labelling them.

Spats   gaiters   farthingale   knickerbockers
bustle   crinoline   semmit   smock

Follow-up
• To learn more about language, see the following unit.
• For help on imaginative writing, see pages 76–77.
• For help on choosing the right register, see pages 32–33.

Spelling Roots and Derivations

- to know more about how roots and derivations of words affect their spellings
- to understand what prefixes and suffixes are

Improving Your Spelling

Most people have at least one or two words that they find difficult to spell. Not everybody has trouble with the same words and different people tackle their problems in different ways. However, one thing is certain: improving your spelling is up to you. Turn learning spellings into something active:

- keep a list or notebook of your own troublesome words
- concentrate on only one or two words a day
- say out loud the word you have trouble spelling
  (Try to pronounce each syllable as well as silent letters if it helps.)
- picture the word in your head, without looking at it on the paper
- trace round each letter in your mind
- once it is fixed in your mind, write the word down from memory
- check that you have got it right
- repeat this process at least three times for each word

To learn spellings: Look Remember Cover Write Check

You could also make up mnemonic (memory-helping) sentences using each letter of problem words:
e.g. SEPARATE = **S**onia **E**ats **P**eas **A**nd **R**adishes **A**t **T**he **E**nd

Choose five words that you have difficulty spelling and make up your own mnemonic sentences.

Activity

Sometimes it can also help to have an idea of where a word has come from in the past – what its roots and derivations are.

1 Many of our words have their roots in Old English, though it is not always easy to see the connection. Can you find the modern words for these?
   - a container for carrying water, etc.
     (from Old English *buc* = a pitcher)
   - a passage between rows of seats
     (from Old English *gangan* = to go)
   - not often
     (from Old English *sel* = rare)
   - to go with the wind or tide
     (from Old English *drifan* = to drive)

2 All the French words listed below have a near relation in the English language. The meanings of the English words are not quite the same as the French words, but the connection is close. Find at least one English word that is similar in spelling and meaning to the French word.
   coucher = to lie down   *langue* = tongue   *malade* = ill
   lune = moon   *laver* = to wash

3 Many of our modern words come straight from Latin or Greek. Although the Ancient Greeks used an alphabet that looks very different from ours, many English words are simply Greek words translated into English letters. The Latin alphabet is the same as English, so some Latin words are the same as English words.

Here is a school timetable completed with the original Greek (Gk) or Latin (L) words, with their translations below. Can you work out what the modern subjects would be?

Monday	*historia* (Gk) enquiry	*physis* (Gk) nature	*ge* (Gk) the earth	*mathema* (Gk) something learned
Tuesday	*bios* (Gk) life	*religio* (L) religion	*computo* (L) I reckon	*physis* (Gk) *educare* (L) nature + to train
Wednesday	*drama* (Gk) doing	*ars* (L) skill	*techne* (Gk) skill	*commercium* (L) trade
Thursday	*mousa* (Gk) arts goddess	*chymeia* (Gk) mixing metals	*studium* (L) study	*scientia* (L) knowledge
Friday	*littera* (L) written	*polis* (Gk) how states work	*botane* (Gk) study of plants	*astron* (Gk) study of stars

Suffixes

A suffix is an ending added on to a base word. Here are some Greek suffixes, which help to create words you will recognize.

-logy   (from the Greek, meaning 'study of') – biology (*bios*+*logy*)

-graphy (from the Greek meaning 'draw' or 'write') – geography (*ge*+*graphy*)

-nomy (from the Greek meaning 'law, order') – astronomy (*astron*+*nomy*)

Prefixes

Parts of a word added at the beginning of a base word are called prefixes. Like suffixes, most prefixes have meanings. Usually, a prefix is added to a base word without changing any letters either in the original word or in the prefix.

Words can be built up with both suffixes and prefixes. Look at the example below:

prefix	**base word**	**suffix**
dis	appear	ance

Activity

1 Try to sort out the prefixes, base words, and suffixes in these words:
unpleasantness   unsympathetic   intercontinental   untruthful

Follow-up

- For more on the origins of words, see pages 22–23.
- For more on spelling patterns, see the following unit.
- To learn about using dictionaries, see pages 28–29.

Word Families

Common Roots

When several words have developed from the same root, their meanings are often alike in some ways. We can think of these words as belonging to the same families.

Activity

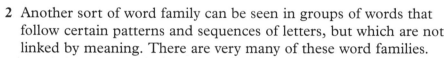

1 From each clue below, try to work out the word being defined. The answers are all linked with the Greek word *monos*, which means alone. If you need help in finding the answers to these, look up the 'mon-'/'mono-' group of words in a dictionary.

- a design of overlapping initials
- where monks live
- the person who reigns
- speech that is in one tone of voice
- one firm only doing a particular kind of business

2 Another sort of word family can be seen in groups of words that follow certain patterns and sequences of letters, but which are not linked by meaning. There are very many of these word families.

Can you add any more words to the families below? How many different families can you find on your own?

beginnings	middles	endings
sch-	*-ou-*	*-ation*
school	trouble	nation
scheme	double	station
scholar	country	ration
schooner	couple	dictation
phys-	*-ee-*	*-age*
physics	sweet	marriage
physician	meet	carriage
physiology	street	baggage
physiotherapy	sheep	damage

3 How many word families can you find that contain silent letters?
e.g. *-gh-* (as in ni*gh*t) *k-* (as in *k*nife) *h-* (as in *h*our)

Regular Patterns

Once you get used to the idea of word families, you will probably become aware of the fact that most words are spelled according to a variety of regular patterns. There are several simple rules that will help you remember them.

Plurals

The word plural means more than one. Most words are made plural by adding -*s*:

> cat – cat*s*   house – house*s*

However there are some exceptions. To make plurals of words ending in -*s*, -*x*, -*ch*, or -*sh*, you need to add -*es*:

> bus – bus*es*   box – box*es*   lunch – lunch*es*   wish – wish*es*

For words ending in -*f*, or -*fe*, it is usual to change the *f* into *v* and then add -*s* or -*es*:

> cal*f* – cal*ves*   li*fe* - li*ves* (exceptions: cliffs, gulfs, chiefs, roofs)

For words ending in -*y* after a vowel, just add -*s:*

> day – day*s*   key – key*s*   boy – boy*s*

For words ending in -*y* after a consonant, change the *y* to *i* and add -*es:*

> lady – lad*ies*   city – cit*ies*   baby – bab*ies*

For words ending in -*o* after another vowel, add -*s:*

> radio – radio*s*   studio – studio*s*

For words ending in -*o* after a consonant, usually add -*es:*

> echo – echo*es*   potato – potato*es* (exceptions: with most musical words, just add -*s*: piano – piano*s*)

Using *ie* or *ei*

If you learn this simple rhyme (on the right) you should be able to avoid some of the most common spelling mistakes.

> *i* before *e*   (br*ie*f, th*ie*f, ch*ie*f, sh*ie*ld)
> – except after *c* –   (c*ei*ling, rec*ei*ve, rec*ei*pt)
> when the sound is 'ee'
>
> (Exceptions: 'seize', 'weird', 'weir')

Doubling letters: adding -*ed* and -*ing*

Have you ever written 'dinning' when you meant 'dining', or 'hopping' when you meant 'hoping'? This simple rule should help you.

When a one-syllable word ends with one vowel followed by one consonant, double the consonant when you add an ending.

> hop – hopped – hopping   bat – batted – batting
> tap – tapped – tapping   rap – rapped – rapping

Otherwise, the consonant is not doubled.

> dine – dined – dining   sprint – sprinted – sprinting
> ask – asked – asking   tape – taped – taping

Dropping the -*e*

With words ending in a silent -*e:*
* when a vowel suffix is added, the -*e* is usually dropped
  > e.g. slic*e* – slicing   lov*e* – loving   separat*e* – separating
* when a consonant suffix is added, the -*e* is not dropped
  > e.g. replac*e* – replacement   spit*e* – spiteful   lon*e* – lonely

Follow-up
* For more help on spelling, see pages 24-25.
* For more on dictionary use, see the following unit.

Dictionary and Vocabulary Skills

Dictionaries

The best way to learn about words is by using a dictionary. It tells us how to spell and pronounce words, what they mean, and what word classes they belong to. Dictionaries can also give examples of how words are used, and some give information about the roots and derivations of words. You must feel confident with alphabetical order if you are going to use a dictionary effectively.

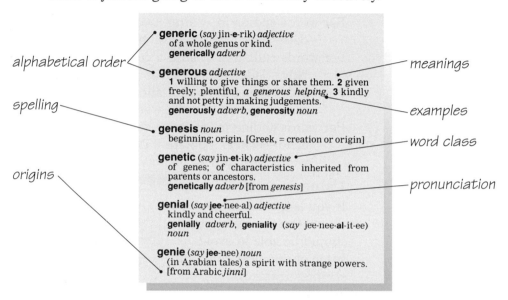

alphabetical order

spelling

origins

meanings

examples

word class

pronunciation

generic (*say* jin-**e**-rik) *adjective*
of a whole genus or kind.
generically *adverb*

generous *adjective*
1 willing to give things or share them. **2** given freely; plentiful, *a generous helping*. **3** kindly and not petty in making judgements.
generously *adverb*, **generosity** *noun*

genesis *noun*
beginning; origin. [Greek, = creation or origin]

genetic (*say* jin-**et**-ik) *adjective*
of genes; of characteristics inherited from parents or ancestors.
genetically *adverb* [from *genesis*]

genial (*say* **jee**-nee-al) *adjective*
kindly and cheerful.
genially *adverb*, **geniality** (*say* jee-nee-al-it-ee) *noun*

genie (*say* **jee**-nee) *noun*
(in Arabian tales) a spirit with strange powers.
[from Arabic *jinni*]

Jabberwocky

'Twas brillig, and the slithy toves
Did gyre and gimble in the wabe:
All mimsy were the borogoves,
And the mome raths outgrabe.

'Beware the Jabberwock, my son!
The jaws that bite, the claws that catch!
Beware the Jubjub bird, and shun
The fruminous Bandersnatch!'

He took his vorpal sword in hand:
Long time the manxome foe he sought–
So rested he by the Tumtum tree,
And stood awhile in thought.

And as in uffish thought he stood,
The Jabberwock, with eyes of flame,
Came whiffling through the tulgey wood,
And burbled as it came!

One, two! One, two! And through and through
The vorpal blade went snicker-snack!
He left it dead, and with its head
He went galumphing back.

'And hast thou slain the Jabberwock?
Come to my arms, my beamish boy!
O frabjous day! Callooh! Callay!'
He chortled in his joy.

'Twas brillig, and the slithy toves
Did gyre and gimble in the wabe;
All mimsy were the borogoves,
And the mome raths outgrabe.

Lewis Carroll

Activity Lewis Carroll made up a lot of the words in his poem *Jabberwocky*. Choose four of them and try to decide what you think they mean. Write full dictionary definitions for each one, following the format of the dictionary entries on page 28 as closely as possible.

Extending Your Vocabulary

You do not necessarily need to invent words to make your writing interesting and lively, but you do need to get into the habit of choosing your words with care. It is a good idea to use a thesaurus if you find yourself stuck for an interesting word. They give lists of words which have similar meanings (synonyms), but take care not to rely too heavily on a thesaurus.

Synonyms and antonyms

If you do not have a thesaurus, you can still become a collector of words. Words that are similar in meaning are called *synonyms*, while their opposites are called *antonyms*.

Activity 1 Some synonyms for cold are listed below. How many more can you find? Use the poem by Laurie Lee as a starting point for your list and include words, phrases, and comparisons.

Raw shivering
biting cutting crystal
chill nipping numb
bleak bitter

Tonight the wind gnaws
with teeth of glass,
the jackdaw shivers
in caged branches of iron,
the stars have talons
Laurie Lee

2 Now collect some antonyms for cold. These will all be words linked with heat. Use the extract from the John Clare poem below as a starting point for your list and include words, phrases, and comparisons.

... noon burns with its blistering breath
Around, and day dies still as death.
...
And in the oven-heated air,
Not one light thing is floating there,
Save that to the earnest eye,
The restless heat seems twittering by.
John Clare

Follow-up • For more on alphabetical order, see page 42.

Accent and Dialect

Objectives:

- to recognize the importance of being able to speak and write in Standard English
- to understand what is meant by accent
- to understand how accent is different from dialect

Standard English

Standard English:
- used to be a dialect from the East Midlands, but it is now the most widely used dialect in England, frequently used on TV and radio
- is so-called because it has certain agreed rules that everyone recognizes – this avoids confusion and makes it the main language of communication
- can be spoken with any regional accent

Any official type of writing or speaking – where you are communicating information to people you may not know – tends to be in Standard English.

Activity

1 Look at the piece of writing below. It is the official report made by some boys who were witnesses to a burglary. The report has been written in Standard English.

> On Tuesday 14th, last week, I was on my way home from school with three of my friends. We saw a man coming towards us – we aren't easily frightened, but he looked very threatening. We didn't see anyone else. There were broken windows over by the cars and an alarm was ringing. We were really scared, so my friends and I just ran away.

2 Now look at the way this report was originally given – informally, in non-standard language. Try to retell this story in your own sort of language, using words and phrases you would use with your friends.

> On Tuesday of last week me and me mates was on our way from school. Well, we sees this man coming towards us – we ain't easily scared, but he were a real hard case. We didn't see no one else. There was broken windows over by them cars and an alarm was ringing. We was real scared, so me and me mates just legged it.

Accent

Accents are differences in the way people from different areas or from different social groupings pronounce words.

Most people pronounce words differently depending on where they come from in the country. An accent belonging to a particular place is called a regional accent, e.g. geordie, cockney, Yorkshire, Lothian. How many more can you think of?

Some people in Britain do not speak with a regional accent. They speak with an accent which does not belong to a particular place. You will find that it is the accent used by many influential people. It is called Received Pronunciation (RP for short, and sometimes known as BBC English).

Working on

1 First of all read aloud the piece below, which has been written in Standard English. Try to begin with Received Pronunciation and then imitate two or three regional accents.

> The summer fair was the last time he ever saw her. She was lost from view among crowds of people pressing round the bottle stall, her hat disappearing from sight with unexpected suddenness.
> 'Oh well, that's life, isn't it?' he sighed.

2 Now try reading this representation of a very posh accent:

> 'Sway thing, Kleddies n Gentlemen, the chew-lolla gree with mih whennay seh, femmay coiner phrezz, we raw linner grimment.' (From *Fraffly Suite* by A. Lauder)
> (So I think, ladies and gentlemen, that you will all agree with me...)

Dialect

Dialects are differences in words and grammar that reveal which country or part of the country a person comes from.
A dialect:

* uses some words that no other dialect uses
* sometimes uses different word and sentence construction (grammar) than Standard English
* is usually spoken in a regional accent

Working on

Read aloud this poem that has been written in a cockney accent and dialect. Then read it a second time, trying to use Received Pronunciation. Can you find Standard English words and phrases for the highlighted dialect parts?

Dahn the Plug 'Ole

A muvver was barfin 'er biby one night,
The youngest of ten and a tiny young mite,
The muvver was poor and the biby was thin,
Only a skelington covered in skin;
The muvver turned rahnd for the soap off the rack,
She was but a moment, but when she turned back,
The biby was gorn; and in anguish she cried,
'Oh, where is my biby?' – The angels replied:

'Your biby 'as fell dahn the plug-'ole,
Your biby 'as gorn dahn the plug;
The poor little thing was so skinny and thin
'E oughter been barfed in a jug;
Your biby is perfeckly 'appy,
'E won't need a barf any more,
Your biby 'as fell dahn the plug 'ole
Not lorst, but gone before.

Anon

Follow-up • For more on formal v. informal language, see the following unit.

Choosing the Right Register

- to understand what we mean when we use the word 'register'
- to be able to choose a way of speaking appropriate to the occasion

Register

Register is what we call the particular way of speaking or writing that belongs to a particular occasion or activity. The register depends on:

- *who* we are talking to – audience
- *why* we are talking to them – purpose
- *what* we are talking about – topic

Activity

Have you ever got it wrong?

It is quite easy to sort out which greeting should match which relationship, but what happens if you get it wrong? Look at the pictures and greetings below. First try matching a greeting to the wrong picture. What would the consequences be? Now match them as you think they should be. What do the greetings show about the relationships?

1 'Hello, Mum'   **4** 'Hello, Mrs Hardy'
2 'Hi, Gramps'   **5** 'Hi, Helen'
3 'Morning, sir'   **6** 'Wotcha, fathead!'

a Parent

b Teacher

c Sister

f Friend

e Grandfather

d Elderly neighbour

We all change the way we speak according to the people we are talking to. Sometimes we just change the tone of voice, but sometimes we change the vocabulary too.

 Working on Look at the following picture story.

Two boys are playing with water pistols in a school corridor.

They do not see a teacher coming round the corner.

One boy ducks to avoid the spray, and the teacher gets it in his face.

They are taken to the Head.

They tell their families what happened.

The next day they tell the story to their friends.

Work out and record what you think the following conversations would be like:
- the angry teacher's reaction to the two boys
- the conversation and explanation to the Head
- the apology to the teacher and the teacher's reply
- the boys telling their families what has happened
- the boys retelling all the events to their friends

Remember to think carefully about:
- *who* you are talking to (your audience)
- *why* you are talking to each other (the purpose of your conversation)
- *what* you are talking about (your topic) and adapt your tone of voice as well as the words you use to make them appropriate to each situation

Follow-up • To learn more about tone and register in speech, see pages 40–41.

Becoming an Effective Speaker

What to Do in Order to Speak Well

Whatever talking activity you have to take part in, you need to make yourself understood by the people listening to you. Many people are very nervous when they have to speak in front of other people, but whether you are:

- taking part in an interview
- giving explanations or descriptions
- reading aloud
- telling a story
- arguing, persuading, or debating
- giving a talk or making a speech

there are many things you can do to help yourself relax.

Vary your pace and intonation

- Put as much expression as you can into your voice.
- Slow down and say things more than once for emphasis.
- Use discourse markers such as 'well/then/so'.
- Make emotional or personal appeals if they seem appropriate.
- Stress words and ideas that are important.

Do not rush

- You are not in a race.
- Take your time to illustrate your points (use handouts/the board).
- But try not to hesitate and stutter, overusing 'fillers' such as 'you know/er/like'.
- Think about punctuation marks which tell you when to pause.

HELP!

Involve your audience

- Keep your head up and look at your audience – smile!
- Do use notes or prompt cards, but don't just read.
- Try to look confident, even if you are really very nervous and embarrassed.
- Use body language, gestures, and eye contact, but don't fidget!
- Try to use some rhetorical devices – address your audience directly.
- Use alliteration, slogans, and comparisons.

Speak clearly and audibly

- Sound your words properly without dropping letters at the beginning, middle, or end of words.
- Avoid using slang in formal situations.
- Try to vary your choice of words.
- Make sure you use plurals and connectives accurately.
- Verbs should be consistent.

Activity Try reading this poem, taking care to pronounce all the consonant sounds clearly.

The Wendigo

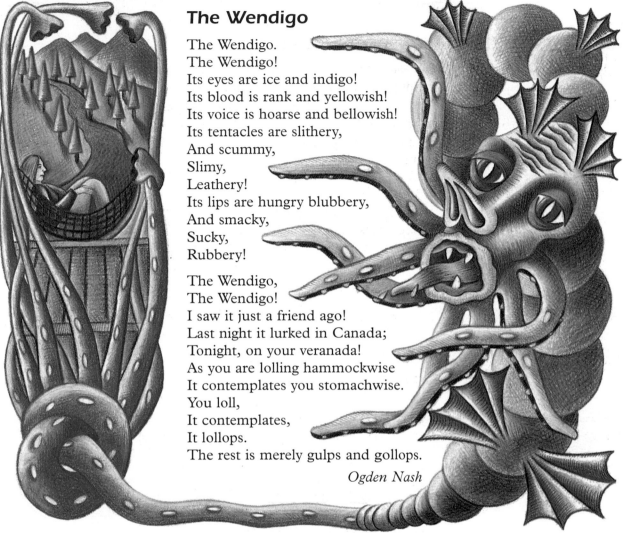

The Wendigo.
The Wendigo!
Its eyes are ice and indigo!
Its blood is rank and yellowish!
Its voice is hoarse and bellowish!
Its tentacles are slithery,
And scummy,
Slimy,
Leathery!
Its lips are hungry blubbery,
And smacky,
Sucky,
Rubbery!

The Wendigo,
The Wendigo!
I saw it just a friend ago!
Last night it lurked in Canada;
Tonight, on your veranada!
As you are lolling hammockwise
It contemplates you stomachwise.
You loll,
It contemplates,
It lollops.
The rest is merely gulps and gollops.

Ogden Nash

Now try to listen to yourself speaking on tape or on video.

1 Choose a page from a book you are reading at the moment either at home or at school. Record yourself reading it aloud. Imagine you are reading to the rest of your class.

2 Now spend some time thinking about what was either the best or the worst day of your life. Record yourself talking about this and try to speak for at least two or three minutes.

When you replay the tapes try to give some thought to how you could improve. Look at the hints outlined on page 34. How many of them were you able to include?

Follow-up
- For help on using verbs, see pages 8–9.
- For help on writing notes, see page 48.
- For help on using connectives, see page 64.
- For help on technical terms, see the Glossary on pages 126–127.

Giving a Talk

- to be able to identify the features that make a powerful, effective speech
- to learn how to plan a speech or talk
- to learn how to give a talk clearly and confidently

Making Speeches

Below is an extract from a famous political speech given in 1963 by Martin Luther King. He was speaking after laws discriminating between black and white citizens in the USA had been repealed.

Although you are only looking at the written words, rather than hearing them spoken, you can still get a good idea of the power of this speech.

I Have a Dream

attempts to involve the audience; speaks personally to his audience

I say to you today, <u>my friends</u>, that in spite of the difficulties and frustrations of the moment I still <u>have a dream</u>. It is a dream deeply rooted in the American dream.

'I have a dream' – saying things more than once for emphasis

<u>I have a dream</u> that one day this nation will rise up and live out the true meaning of its creed: 'We hold these truths to be self-evident; that all men are equal.'

emotional appeal

<u>I have a dream</u> that one day on the red hills of Georgia the sons of <u>former slaves</u> and the sons of <u>former slave-owners</u> will be able to sit down together at the table of brotherhood ...

appealing on a personal level

<u>I have a dream</u> that <u>my four little children</u> will one day live in a Nation where they will not be judged by the **c**olour of their skins, but by their **c**onduct and their **c**haracter.

'c' – alliteration for effect

language from the Bible to add weight

<u>I have a dream</u> that one day ... every valley shall be exalted, every hill and mountain shall be made low, the crooked places will be made straight and the glory of the Lord shall be revealed ...

strong emotional appeal plus repetition of the words 'hope', 'faith', and 'together'

This is our <u>hope</u>. This is the <u>faith</u> that I go back to the South with. With this <u>faith</u>, we will be able to hew out of mountains of despair a stone of <u>hope</u>. With this <u>faith</u>, we will be able to transform the jangling discord of our Nation into a beautiful symphony of brotherhood. With this <u>faith</u>, we will be able to work <u>together</u>; to go to jail <u>together</u>; to stand up for freedom <u>together</u> knowing that we will be free one day ...

It might not be appropriate for you to give a talk like that, but there are things you can learn from it.

Although it can be a nerve-racking experience giving a talk to your class, careful preparation will help you. Clearly, giving a talk like the one on the next page is hardly worth the effort. How many things can you find wrong with it?

I'm going to talk to you about fishing. Um ... I ... um go fishing every weekend with um ... a couple of me mates and um it's a bit of a laugh, you know. Um ... you can get a bit cold sometimes, you know, um ... when you're out all night, like. But it's all right, really. Um ... I've never caught much but it's well cool. Um ... I ain't got no more to say, miss.

What should I talk about?

Make sure your talk is about:

- something you are interested in
- something which you know a good deal about
- something you enjoy
- something you have strong views about

How do I plan?

To plan your talk:

- carry out any research you might need to do
- write out your talk in detail but remember that eventually you will be giving a talk not a reading
- check you have a lively opening and a strong conclusion and that you have avoided clichés
- develop your ideas in carefully structured paragraphs
- summarize each paragraph in a few words
- write these on small cards to use in your talk
- prepare props to help you, but not too many – diagrams, posters, souvenirs, etc.
- know your speech thoroughly

On the day

When the time to give your talk finally comes:

- relax by breathing slowly and deeply before you start
- look at your audience and smile
- do not rely too heavily on your notes – they should be used as reminders only
- be interesting and confident
- put as much expression into your voice and face as you can
- use your hands to emphasize what you are saying
- do not rush!

Activity Now choose a topic and prepare a ten minute talk. It could be about a holiday, a hobby, a job, your family, an issue. When you have finished your preparation, practise by recording yourself on tape.

Follow-up
- For help on making notes and summarizing, see pages 48–49.
- For help on structuring and sequencing paragraphs, see pages 20–21.
- For help on choosing the appropriate tone and language, see pages 32–33.

Becoming an Effective Listener

Careful Listening

Good listening is a skill that can be developed and improved. We all need to listen to try to understand the thoughts and feelings of others. We need to be able to interpret the way words are spoken as well as what is said.

In a world that is full of sound and noise, hearing is taken very much for granted. You do not need to listen carefully to everything you can hear, but you do need to know when you should listen carefully.

Activity

Stop what you are doing now and listen carefully to all the sounds around you – the sorts of sounds you normally hear but do not necessarily listen to. List them. Now make a list of six of your favourite sounds and contrast them with six sounds you do not like.

John Cotton has made a poem out of the sounds he can hear in the kitchen:

In the Kitchen

In the kitchen
After the aimless
Chatter of the plates,
The murmurings of the gas,
The chuckle of the water pipes
And the sharp exchanges
Of knives, forks and spoons,
Comes the serious quiet,
When the sink slowly clears its throat
And you can hear the occasional rumble
Of the refrigerator's tummy
As it digests the cold.

John Cotton

What Stops You Being a Good Listener?

How many of these reasons apply to you? Can you think of any more?

The subject is dull and boring.

You pretend to listen.

You are distracted by people around you.

You day-dream.

You are distracted by how the speaker looks and behaves.

Other noises intrude.

You switch off if you find the topic hard

The speaker's voice is monotonous.

You are too busy trying to catch every word.

Active Listening

Listen to the news on TV and try to summarize the main points of what you have heard. You won't be able to remember all the facts and details, so concentrate on the key points.

CHECKLIST FOR WATCHING THE NEWS

Your listening skills:
- What was the main news item?
- What were the main details of this story?
- Was the voice audible and clear?
- Was it relevant and interesting?

The presenter's listening skills:
- In interviews, did the interviewer listen to others?
- Did the interviewer respond to what was said, or just use prepared questions?
- Did anything distract you?
- What elements made it interesting?

Activity

1 Imagine your local Post Office has just been raided by armed robbers.
- What was stolen?
- Were there any injuries?
- How many robbers were there?
- What did they look like?
- How did they get away?

Plan, perform, and record this as a news item.

2 Ask a parent or grandparent what life and school were like when they were young. It might help to prepare questions and tape this as an interview, but be prepared to make up spontaneous questions to follow-up on interesting answers. Try to remember the following points:
- listen expecting to hear something interesting
- listen to what they say rather than the way they are saying it
- jot down key ideas while you are listening
- concentrate hard
- keep an open mind and do not jump to conclusions
- work hard at being an active listener

3 Now use the information from your interview to prepare a talk on the differences between being a child now and in the past. Tape your talk and then listen to it.

Follow-up
- For more help on giving a talk, see pages 36–37.

Ways of Presenting Speech

Objectives:

- to understand the main differences between speech and writing
- to be able to write in script form
- to learn how to present direct and indirect speech

Writing Down What People Say

Talk is usually something you do with other people and unless it is recorded or remembered, it is lost. When they are talking, people repeat themselves, hesitate, depend on gestures, facial expressions, and tone of voice. If you try and write down exactly what they say, you find it is quite hard to understand.

Speech is very different from the written word, which stays fixed on the page and depends on punctuation and grammar for its meaning. There are several forms of writing which show what people say: transcript, script, direct speech, and indirect speech. They are presented differently and are used for different purposes.

Transcript

A transcript is an exact copy of what is said. Look at the following conversation.

Language is often informal and is not structured in complete sentences.

You can hear pauses and hesitations.

It's hard to see where another person is speaking but it's easy to hear it.

Scuse me um sorry to bother you ... but can you tell me which way for the mill / no problem um let's see you go down there that way you're heading in the wrong direction completely so turn round straight along for a bit um lets see ... take the next left past the lights then right / no that's not right at all if you want to get to the main car park you're right as you are look ... take the next right right again through two sets of lights then left by the pub it's easy / thanks very much I'm sure I'll find it now

Script

Script is another way of showing conversation in writing. It is normally used for plays. Continue the conversation in script form.

Information to set the scene and give stage directions is in italics.

The names of the characters are at the left of the page, followed by a colon.

The speech is written without quotation marks.

The scene is a fairly busy street on a wet and windy winter's day. A harassed and puzzled motorist can be seen in a car, peering with despair at a map. The motorist gets out of the car and goes up to a man and a lady who are walking past. They are cold and wet and anxious to be on their way.

Motorist: (*Hesitantly*) Excuse me! I'm sorry to bother you, but can you tell me which way for The Mill?

Man: No problem ... um (*Slight pause while he thinks*). Let's see. You go down there, that way. (*He points in the opposite direction to which the motorist is facing.*)

Information about characters is put in brackets in italics.

Direct Speech

Direct speech is most commonly found in stories. One of the main differences between direct speech, script, or transcript is in the punctuation. Using the information in the transcript on page 40, continue the conversation below in direct speech.

Where something happens it should be written as part of the story.

Each new piece of speech must begin with a capital letter.

Words spoken are enclosed in inverted commas.

For each new speaker start a new line and indent.

> The car pulled to a halt alongside a newsagent shop. Chris was breathing heavily by now, anxious to look at the map. After some minutes, and being none the wiser, Chris decided it was time to stop being so independent, and ask for help. He struggled out of the car and was buffeted by the full force of the wind and rain.
>
> 'Excuse me,' he said hesitantly to a couple who were hurrying past, clearly anxious to get home, 'but can you tell me which way for The Mill?'

Each piece of speech must end with a full stop, a question mark or an exclamation mark before the closing inverted comma.

When a spoken sentence is interrupted it continues <u>without</u> a capital letter.

Indirect Speech

Direct speech gives us a record of words actually spoken, but indirect speech is what we are told when someone is reporting what was said. It can also be called reported speech. Continue the conversation below in indirect speech.

All verbs change to the past tense.

First person pronoun changes to third person.

> Chris approached a couple hesitantly and said that he was sorry to have bothered them. He wondered if they could tell him which way he would have to go to get to The Mill. They said that they could and proceeded to give him instructions. The man began by telling Chris that he had been going in completely the wrong direction.

Instead of words actually spoken, 'that' introduces a report of them.

Activity

1 Now try some transcribing of speech for yourself. Tape a short, natural conversation and then try to write down everything that was said, e.g. a parent asking who wants to eat what for an evening meal, or friends discussing their favourite TV programme, etc.
Note: Include all the pauses such as 'um's, and 'er's.

2 Now turn it into direct speech. You might need to cut parts out as well as making some changes or additions. You will also need to add the correct punctuation.

3 The next task is to see if you can report this conversation in indirect speech. You will need to write in the third person and make sure that all the verbs are in the past tense. You might need to add words such as 'whether' if you are reporting a question.

Follow-up • For more help on playscripts, see pages 104–105.

Skimming and Scanning

- to understand that different methods of reading can be used when reading for information
- to develop the fast-reading skills of skimming and scanning

Skimming for Information

Skimming is a way of reading very quickly when you do not need to read all the words carefully. You let your eyes run quickly over the words on a page, trying to get a general impression of the contents.

Activity

Skimming through lists

1 Skim the index below, timing yourself to see how quickly you can find the page number where information about the following birds can be found:

Fieldfare   Buzzard   Gannet   Falcon   Chaffinch
Grebe   Dipper   Bunting   Corncrake   Eagle

ENTERTAINMENT

SKY ONE

7.00-8.30am Boiled Egg and Soldiers Featuring: 7.05 X-Men 8641592 8.00 Mighty Morphin Power Rangers 3469384 8.25 Dennis 4526636 8.30 Press Your Luck 5495742 8.50 Love Connection 4610029 9.20 Court TV 6703891 9.50 The Oprah Winfrey Show 1240100 10.40 Jeopardy! 6507810 11.10 Sally Jessy Raphael 2342181 12.00noon Beechy 96568 1.00pm Hotel 72988 2.00 Geraldo 43075 3.00 Court TV 3902 3.30 The Oprah Winfrey Show 5310988 4.15 Mighty Morphin Power Rangers 7707181 4.40 X-Men 2078013

5.00 Star Trek: The Next Generation Sci-fi drama series. Troi, Riker and Dr Crusher all fall into a coma. 4742
6.00 The Simpsons Lisa wins a competition writing about patriotism. 8433
6.30 Jeopardy! 2013
7.00 LAPD Fly-on-the-wall documentary series. 5471
7.30 M*A*S*H A bomb lands in the camp just as the 4077th are settling down to listen to the army-navy football game. 8297
8.00 Central Park West Drama series. Nikki runs to Peter after she discovers telephone bugs and hidden video cameras in her gallery and apartment. 35471
9.00 Police Rescue Drama series set in Australia. A mistake by Georgia puts the lives of two children in danger. 22907
10.00 Star Trek: The Next Generation See 5.00pm. 25094
11.00 Melrose Place Drama series. Michael tries to convince Kimberly that he really loves her. But will she

UK GOLD

7.00am Angels 3608079 7.30 Neighbours 4153164 8.00 Sons and Daughters 7685568 8.30 EastEnders 7684839 9.00 The Bill 7668891 9.30 The Sullivans 2194433 10.00 Secret Army 8753128 11.00 One Out 2003907 12.05pm Sons and Daughters 38881094 12.30 Neighbours 2105549 1.00 EastEnders 3653568 1.35 Sykes 1441013 2.15 Man About the House 1168839 2.50 Three Up, Two Down 7785346 3.30 The Bill 6398433 4.00 Casualty 2238100 5.00 Every Second Counts 3890758 5.45 'Allo 'Allo 1920075
6.25 EastEnders 6854988
7.00 The Two Ronnies Comedy series. 9487346
8.00 Bullseye 4107029
8.30 Man About the House 4013636
9.00 Casualty Jon Rowdon tries to bolster his own confidence 9589758
10.00 The Bill The husband of Roach's girlfriend is released from jail. 1906452
10.35 Top of the Pops With ABBA, The Bay City Rollers, The Drifters and Kiki Dee from 1976. 6889278
11.15 Widows The women are ready for the raid – but will they succeed where their husbands failed? 8679433
12.15am FILM: Baby Face Morgan Comedy starring Virginia Carlisle and Richard Cromwell. (1942) 8161105
1.15-1.45am Bless This House 5834124

SCI-FI Available on cable 8.00am-2.00am, and also on Astra 7.00pm-10.00pm and 1.00am-4.00am:
8.00am Knightmare. 8.25 Space Angel. 8.35 G-Force. 9.00 A

Index

Bittern **153**	Coot **219**	Diver **205**	Gadwall **135**
Blackbird **11**	Cormorant **118**	Dotterel **179**	Gannet **121**
Blackcap **23**	Corncrake **215**	Dove **220**	Garganey **136**
Brambling **66**	Crake **215**	Duck **130**	Goldcrest **30**
Bullfinch **60**	Creeper **42**	Dunlin **162**	Goldeneye **143**
Bunting **74**	Crow **70**	Eider **108**	Goldfinch **63**
Buzzard **111**	Crossbill **93**	Eagle **144**	Goosander **148**
Capercaillie **229**	Cuckoo **99**	Falcon **112**	Goose **126**
Chaffinch **63**	Dabchick **171**	Fieldfare **9**	Grebe **211**
Chiffchaff **24**	Curlew **212**	Flycatcher **52**	Greenfinch **59**
Chough **90**	Dipper **33**	Fulmar **202**	Greenshank **172**

2 Words in an index should be in alphabetical order. There are three words that are out of their correct order in the index above. You will need to check alphabetical order according to their first, second, and third letters. Can you find the three words in less than a minute?

Skimming through charts

3 Spend no more than two minutes to skim the Satellite listings on the left and produce a selection of programmes for:
- someone who loves soap operas
- someone who loves comedies

Scanning Longer Passages

Scanning is another way of reading rapidly, when you are looking for a specific detail. Sometimes we need to scan text quickly to see if the information we want is there. With practice you can scan a page until you find a particular piece of information you want. At that point you stop scanning and read more carefully.

Activity

Look at the information below about some of the well-known characters in Shakespeare. Find the answers to the questions below by skimming through the information as fast as you can until you come to the fact you are looking for. Can you answer all the questions within two minutes?

- How many kings are mentioned?
- Who are the ghosts that are mentioned?
- What are the names of the three sisters in King Lear?
- How was Hamlet's father killed?
- Who foretells Macbeth's future?
- What is the name of Polonius's son?
- Who does Cordelia marry?

HAMLET (*Hamlet*): the Prince of Denmark, son of the recently dead King Hamlet and his wife Queen Gertrude. Although Hamlet was the legitimate successor to the throne, he has been excluded from succession by his uncle, Claudius, who has become King in his place having married Hamlet's mother, Gertrude, with great speed. The ghost of Hamlet's father tells him that he was not killed by a snake bite, as had been believed, but poisoned by Claudius. Hamlet then determines to avenge the crime.

BANQUO (*Macbeth*): a Scottish nobleman who is returning with Macbeth having fought against the Norwegians. Together, they encounter three witches who prophesy that Macbeth will be King, but that Banquo will be the founder of a dynasty of kings. Soon after, Macbeth has Banquo murdered and his ghost appears at Macbeth's feast.

LEAR, KING (*King Lear*): the King of Britain during some far distant period of the island's history. When he grows old, Lear decides to divide his kingdom between his three daughters. Goneril and Regan, the two eldest daughters, loudly protest their love for him, but Cordelia, who is more sincere and honest, fails to please her father with what she says, and is deprived of her share. She marries the King of France and leaves the country and Lear is left to the evil greed of his two elder daughters.

OPHELIA (*Hamlet*): the daughter of Polonius and the sister of Laertes. She is in love with Hamlet, even though both her father and brother have told her not to take him seriously. Hamlet starts to behave strangely and Ophelia concludes that he must be mad. She goes mad herself when she hears that Hamlet has killed her father, and is subsequently found drowned.

Follow-up
- For help on reading for detail, see the following unit.
- For help on reading for meaning, see pages 46–47.
- For help on reading Shakespeare, see pages 102–103.

Reading for Detail

Noticing Details

Sometimes you only need to get the general impression, the main ideas, in what you are reading, but if you are reading instructions or information, details become much more important. Noticing small details – sometimes just one word – takes practice and concentration.

This skill involves slow reading. You might need to read parts of sentences and single words, and expect to have to go back and check, rereading parts you might not be sure about.

Activity

1 Read all the following instructions carefully before you begin to write. Then follow the advice above to answer the questions.
   1. Print your name in full, last name first, in block capitals.
   2. Write your address, leaving out the name of your road or street.
   3. Now write the name of your road or street backwards.
   4. Write out the following letters in two columns, the vowels in a column at the extreme left of the page, the consonants at the extreme right of the page:
      p k e h i d n u s w a g t o l
   5. Now, keeping the letters in the same columns, rearrange them into alphabetical order. Write out the new columns in between the original columns.
   6. If you are a girl or a boy between the ages of 11 and 14, do none of the above.
   7. If you have followed instruction 6, write 'yes'; if not, write 'no'.

2 Read the paragraph below.

   For a long time men, women, boys, and girls have taken part in the annual pancake race. Although it can hardly be classed as dangerous, it is good fun and very exciting. Strangely, the number of young girl racers has fallen in the last few years. But there has been a pancake race every spring for over a hundred years and a great many people take part. The main requirements are that you have to be able to make a good pancake, and run with it, and try to beat all the others.

The main idea of this paragraph is concerned with a pancake race. Can you fill in the details?
• Who takes part in the race?
• How often does it take place?
• For how many years has it been taking place?
• What qualities do the people taking part need?
• What has happened to the young girl racers?

Working on Read the following extract, and try to illustrate the details that are described when the boy reaches the junction of the two main roads. You could also work out your version of a map showing the route the boy followed.

Gumble's Yard

Going from the station I soon found the tram-stop. I had a few coppers but decided not to take the tram, because I didn't know what stop to ask for, and I had a dread of arousing suspicion. But I followed the lines, and was soon trudging along the main road, remembering landmarks as I went. So far so good.

Over the bridge with the black waters of the Ledder river beneath; yes, I remembered that. Past Pollards' engineering works; yes, that was right. Then the Bethesda Chapel, sooty as ever. I was doing splendidly. I had a moment's doubt when I came to the junction of two main roads; which should I take? But far along one of them I recognized the sign of the strangely named pub, the Bear and Pineapple, where I remembered that Uncle Bob used to have an occasional glass of beer. And beside the Bear and Pineapple, when I reached it, I recognized the sloping side-street we used to walk down from Uncle's house.

Up the slope I went. I felt confident. At the top was a bare patch of ground; now a row of posts and an entrance to an alley-way that led to a parallel street. I had only to go to the end and turn right and I would see my uncle's house. I knew I was right. There was no possibility of mistake. I almost ran along that last street, and rounded the final corner. And then I gasped with dismay. Instead of the row of houses where my uncle had lived, there was only a bare, black cindery site, with a few oddments of rubbish on it.

John Rowe Townsend

Follow-up • For help on fast-reading techniques, see pages 42–43.
• For help on reading for meaning, see the following unit.

Reading for Meaning

Fact and Opinion

It's not always easy to pick out facts from opinions. Often people say that they are stating facts when they have not checked to see if what they are saying is really true.

- A *fact* is something that can be proved to be true.
  e.g. The local newsagent shuts at 8 p.m.
- An *opinion* is what one, or more than one, person thinks about something.
  e.g. The manager of the newsagent is always grumpy.

Activity

1 Separate the facts from the opinions below.
- Everybody likes chocolate.
- Gemma is the best singer in the school.
- Christmas Day was on a Sunday in 1994.
- Nobody likes to eat eels!
- The Queen owns several dogs.

2 Read the description below, which has been designed to tempt holiday-makers to a particular resort.

The Holiday Resort of your Dreams!

The jewel of the south, this holiday resort will meet all your dreams: a rugged, tumbling rocky coast, sheltering golden, sandy beaches, lapped by shimmering blue bays, set against a background of whispering pine trees. Who could want for more? While the rocky inlets provide secluded, sheltered sunbathing under clear blue skies where the sun always shines, the shimmering, sapphire bays will tempt you to swim in the world's warmest, bluest waters.

Common sense should tell us that all of the details in this piece cannot possibly always be true. The drawbacks have been left out, and facts have been mixed in with opinions. It is your task to try and separate them again. Draw up your own chart. First list all the facts – the things that can be proved to be true – then list the opinions.

3 Choose a place that you feel you could write about – it might be a favourite holiday spot, or perhaps a special place that you used to go to when you were younger. Write your own description of the place, to try to tempt people to visit. Start by making a list of all the facts about the place. Once you have all your information, write a description of your place, and try to weave in your own feelings and opinions about it.

Bias and Objectivity

There are facts and opinions combined in the following articles about Point Horror books. Neither writer stands back from the subject to let you, the reader, make up your own mind – neither one is *objective*. When someone has a particular point of view like this, we call it *bias*. You can be biased in favour of something or against it.

Activity

1 Pick out the particular words and phrases that illustrate the bias of both reviewers below.

Pointless Horror?

It all started with Christopher Pike. The teen horror novel is here with a vengeance ... So, what do you get when you start reading? ... Much of what I read was instantly forgettable but the bits that have stuck seem to have formed themselves into a jelly-like, amorphous mass ...

That's it, then. Cardboard characters (and that's insulting cardboard) acting in banal plots that are riddled with implausibility.

These books are essentially undemanding reads; big print, short chapters, one central plot, little description and plenty of action ... one will be similar to the last.

Steve Rosson

Christopher Pike – Master of Murder

Scary? Teenagers on both sides of the Atlantic seem to think so ... the story is tense and gripping, the settings exciting, and the story concludes with a furious ending that's action-packed without becoming unrealistic ...

Christopher Pike is probably one of the most original and exciting authors of teenage fiction this decade. His writing is flawless, his ideas breath-taking, and there's a mystique about him that's hard to pinpoint. He knows what his readers want and never fails to deliver.

Jonathan Weir

2 Now try writing your own report or review. You could write about a football match, a book, a recent album, a film, or a school production.

First write an account which includes only facts – an objective report/review. Then write a second account where you add words and phrases which show you are biased against your topic. Finally, write a third account where you try to make everything sound as attractive as possible – where you are biased in favour of your topic.

3 Try to analyse what you have done and write a reflective paragraph which describes how you have achieved different effects. Explain what words and phrases you used to influence the reader of your account.

Follow-up

- For help on imaginative writing, see pages 76–77.
- For more practice writing about facts, see pages 70–71.
- For more help on writing persuasively, see pages 66–67.

Note-making and Summary Skills

Making Notes

In many subjects and situations at school, from researching a project to listening to a teacher, you will need to be able to make notes. This does not mean rapidly scribbled jottings, but carefully chosen key words to help you remember what you have heard or read.

Many people write too much when they make notes while researching a project, and rely on copying out chunks of books from here and there. Ideally, you should aim to do the following:

- try to get a grasp of the main idea by skim-reading the passage
- write down the key words of the main ideas, preferably numbering them
- leave out unnecessary words and examples
- use your own words as much as possible

Activity

1 Look at the following short paragraph and try to reduce it to a few key words and ideas.

> Holidaymakers fled for their lives from Brighton promenade yesterday, when a car veered out of control and mounted the pavement after the driver had been taken ill at the wheel. It finally came to a halt after colliding with two other cars and crashing into a lamp-post. Five people were taken to hospital suffering from shock and minor cuts and bruises. The driver, Mr Harry Thomas, aged 69, is now recovering in hospital.

2 Write down what you think the main idea of the paragraph is. If you find this hard to do, it might help you to imagine you have got to write a newspaper headline for the paragraph. Aim for no more than five or six words.

3 Now write numbered notes, mentioning all the main points. Try to use your own wording as far as possible.

Writing a Summary

Summaries are shorter versions of something that has been said or written. They are used in newspaper headlines to give readers some idea of what an article is about; they are used on the backs of books to give an outline of the story; and you may be asked to use them in school, e.g. summarizing the results of a scientific experiment.

The starting point for any summary is being able to make effective notes, ensuring that all the main points have been covered. These are then reworked in your own words.

Activity The following extract is about 150 words long. Try to write a summary of it in no more than 50 words, using the steps outlined on page 48.

The Ghost of Thomas Kempe

It was a golden afternoon. The hedgerows lay in neat black lines among bleached fields of stubble and sunshine came through them in spurts. Long black fingers of shade streamed away from the elms on the hilltop and the whole wide arc of the horizon was fringed with the blue and graceful shapes of trees against the pale sky. James walked along an overgrown lane, between margins rusty with docks and the fine tracery of dried cow-parsley heads, and before long, Arnold came to join him and together they went into the copse by the farm and ate blackberries while Tim and Palmerston rooted in the undergrowth and pigeons lumbered overhead. Arnold knew a place where there'd once been a quarry: it was all green and bushy now, but you could slide down the steep sides and swing Tarzan-like among branches from one side to the other.

Penelope Lively

Working on Good instructions require writing that is concise and to the point.

Think of a card game or a sport that you know how to play.
- Write down the instructions as clearly as you can.
- Concentrate on each main step.
- Produce an illustrated leaflet to explain the rules of your game to a child.

Follow-up
- For help on skim-reading, see pages 42–43.
- For more help on note-making, planning, and drafting, see pages 62–63.

Diaries

Why People Write Diaries

Many people never expect their diaries to be read. They write, usually every day, for themselves, about largely private and personal experiences. People write diaries for all sorts of reasons:

- to record facts
- to chart emotions, hopes, and despairs
- to catch events of day-to-day life
- to describe the passing seasons and surroundings
- to remember important personal or public events
- to share experiences

Diaries help us to see vividly what is being described but at the same time tell us something about the person and personality of the author.

Activity Look at the following diary extracts all written in the month of October.

1　What can you tell about the person who wrote each extract?
2　What sort of life do you think each person led?
3　What do you think is the purpose of each diary?

---

3 October 1783
The cat frolicks, and plays with the fallen leaves, Acorns innumerable.

4 October 1779
Mushrooms abound. Made catchup.

8 October 1791
Earthed up the celeri, which is very gross and large.

---

4 October 1934

A violent rainstorm on the pond. The pond is covered with little white thorns; springing up and down: the pond bristling with leaping white thorns, like thorns on a small porcupine; bristles; then black waves; cross it; black shudders; and the little water thorns are white; a helter skelter rain and the elms tossing it up and down...

---

13 October 1975
Spent all morning rehearsing for the first scene of Hamlet – four hours – and it was a wonderful experience. It's really why I do this job. Not for performances – not for plays – not for money – but for the satisfaction of having a really good rehearsal where the excitement of discovery spreads from actor to actor.

Fictional Diaries

The extracts below are from a book made up of fictional diary entries. This sort of writing suggests that the characters involved are real people and that the events described have actually happened. However, they are entirely imaginary. The author of the extracts is, in fact, a teacher concerned with child protection. She has written several other books for young children.

Everybody else does! Why can't I?

(Diary entry for Jenny, a 14-year-old school girl)

8th October

I was really cut up when David Slater dropped me for Sadie. Funny thing is, I can't for the life of me work out why, now. He's a creep! We only split about three months ago, and he's been out with and dropped two other girls since then. Sadie and I were both taken for a ride. He smiled at me today, all melting marshmallow and gooey charm. I ignored him.

(Diary entry for Jenny's mum)

8th October

Jenny seems to have made up with her friend Sadie. She has a very forgiving nature; I would find it difficult to trust my best friend if she'd been going out with my boyfriend behind my back. When Sadie came round, a bit shame faced, I expected Jenny to give her the heave-ho in no uncertain terms. After an initial frost they ended up chatting away nineteen to the dozen. They're going out together at the weekend: very civilized.

Yvonne Coppard

Activity
- Why do you think the author has written the book in the form of diary entries?
- What impressions do you get of (a) Jenny (b) her mum?
- What sorts of problems are they each faced with?
- What might you learn from a book like this?

Working on
1 Try writing your own diary every day for at least a week. You will not be able to write down everything that happens to you, but concentrate on some of the more interesting things or emotions that you experience from day to day. By the time you have finished, you will have a snapshot picture of yourself and your world.
2 Now develop this diary into a fictional, imaginary version, where you take on a particular personality and do all of the things you really would have liked to have done in that week.
3 Write a short commentary on what you like about each form. Do you prefer one over the other?

Follow-up
- For more on autobiography, see the following unit.
- For help on imaginative writing, see pages 76–77.

Autobiography

What is Autobiography?

An autobiography means writing about your own life. Like a diary, it is a personal piece of writing, but whereas diaries tend to be unshaped and spontaneous, autobiographies tend to be more carefully put together. They are usually written for other people to read. Like diaries, they give us a mixture of information about:
• the person who is writing
• the sort of life that person has had

Activity   Read the following extract from an autobiography by Paul Watkins. When he was seven he was sent to boarding school in Oxford from his home in America. In the extract, he describes one vividly remembered event.

Stand Before Your God

The dorm lights hadn't been off for more than 15 minutes when it was decided that we would have to raid the dorm downstairs. I had been asleep, but now with a dorm raid about to start, I knew there'd be no chance of trying to doze through that ...

An adult might not think there'd be much in the way of weaponry in a dormitory room for seven-year-old boys. But the way we saw it, everything was a weapon. And no excuse was too small for taking your pillow and slamming it down on your next-door-neighbour's head. There were other weapons, too. Slippers. Blankets. Entire mattresses could be used against the enemy.

It was decided that Bosom would open the attack by sliding down the stairs on a mattress. Bosom was not in agreement on this, so he was tied to that mattress with several linked-together belts. And a sock was put in his mouth to discourage any lack of fighting spirit.

Paul Watkins

1 What can you tell about the school from this extract? What can you tell about the boys? Using all the details in the extract, rewrite this piece as if it were an entry in Paul Watkins's diary.

In the extract below from another autobiography, Barbara Windsor remembers a lot of details about all sorts of things.

Barbara: The Laughter and Tears of a Cockney Sparrow

They called me Barbara after the nurse, and Ann after an ice-skating star ... So there I was, Barbara-Ann Deeks, seven pounds of joy.

The doors were never locked in Angela Street and all us kids used to play in the cobblestone street. You seldom heard a car, it was mostly the coalman or the rag-and-bone man with his horse and cart. Whenever the rag-and-bone man appeared, all the kids would scuttle indoors to fetch empty jam jars. Washed clean, they'd fetch a halfpenny to buy sweets from the corner shop. Rags as well meant a goldfish. Our house was always spotless. The smell and the glow of Mansion polish was as familiar as the hopscotch patterns chalked over the pavements. The front doorstep was scrubbed every day, whatever the weather. Each family had a zinc bath, usually brought into the kitchen and placed in front of the boiler where I'd be given a good scrub down after a boisterous day's play.

In the outside loo the newspaper was cut into neat little squares, threaded with string and hung on a nail. They knew how to treat the tabloids in those days!

Barbara Windsor

2 Write a list of the different things Barbara Windsor remembers.
3 Now make a written comparison between *Stand Before Your God* and *Barbara: The Laughter and Tears of a Cockney Sparrow*. Compare how the authors have shared their remembered details. What effects do they have on a reader?

Working on

What are your early memories like? Choose your own favourite memory. Perhaps you can remember a complete event like Paul Watkins, or maybe you can remember lots of small details like Barbara Windsor.

1 Write your memory as clearly and accurately as you can.
2 Now write it again, deliberately trying to entertain or amuse the person reading it. Add an explanation of what you changed and why you changed it.

Follow-up
- For help on setting and atmosphere, see pages 88–89.
- To learn more about the author's point of view, see pages 92–93.
- For help on reading prose, see pages 96–97.

Maps, Charts, and Graphs

Objectives:

- to improve your understanding of maps
- to practise interpreting graphs and charts
- to learn how to use information to develop a point of view

Maps

Sometimes information is easier to understand when it is shown visually – in pictures, maps, graphs, or charts.

Look at the maps on this page, which show the site of a possible new runway at Gatwick Airport. The one below is a close-up view and the one on the right shows a larger area.

    On the close-up map, which places would be most affected by a new runway? How would they be affected?

    On the map which shows a larger area, explain the changes that would need to be made to roads, housing, and railways if the runway was built.

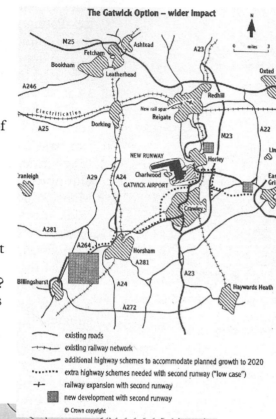

The Gatwick Option – wider impact

         — existing roads
         —+— existing railway network
         ⋯⋯ additional highway schemes to accommodate planned growth to 2020
         ⋯⋯ extra highway schemes needed with second runway ("low case")
         —+— railway expansion with second runway
         ▨ new development with second runway
         © Crown copyright

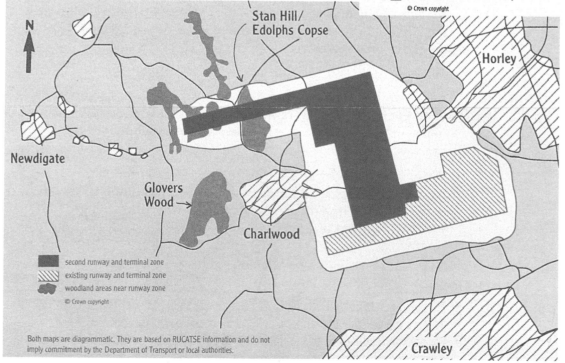

■ second runway and terminal zone
▨ existing runway and terminal zone
▩ woodland areas near runway zone
© Crown copyright

Both maps are diagrammatic. They are based on RUCATSE information and do not imply commitment by the Department of Transport or local authorities.

Charts

It is estimated that an extra 27,000 houses would need to be built to accommodate the workers on the new runway. Some suggested sites include the following:

Possible site	Extra houses needed
North of Horley	4,000
Between Crawley and East Grinstead	3,000
South-west of Horsham	20,000

Bar Graph

Large areas of land would be lost, including Green Belt land and land for building.

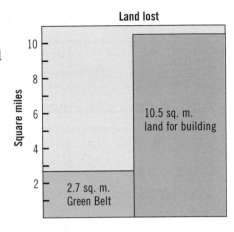

Land lost

Additional information

- There would be a fourfold rise in passengers (to 80 million each year).
- Road and rail links would be developed over a wide area.
- A large part of Stan Hill would need to be removed.
- The village of Charlwood would be isolated between two runways.
- Houses would be demolished or would become uninhabitable.
- There would be more noise and pollution for communities near the airport.
- There would be more jobs both in and around the airport.
- People directly affected by a new runway should be able to claim compensation.

Activity

Write two different reports using all the information that you have about the proposed new runway. Include maps and charts of your own if it helps to make your written reports clearer.

1 Report 1 should be from the point of view of someone in favour of the runway trying to persuade others that it would be a good idea.

2 Report 2 should be from the point of view of someone opposed to the runway trying to persuade others to mount a campaign against it.

Follow-up

- For help on writing persuasively, see pages 66–67.
- For advice on planning and drafting, see pages 62–63.

Advertising

Objectives:

- to understand more about how to read an advertisement
- to produce and analyse your own advert

Reading Advertisements

In our everyday lives we are surrounded by advertisements all trying to sell us something – on TV, on the radio, in magazines, and in newspapers. But have you ever stopped to think about the way they are put together and how they work? Have you ever thought:

What is this advertisement really saying?

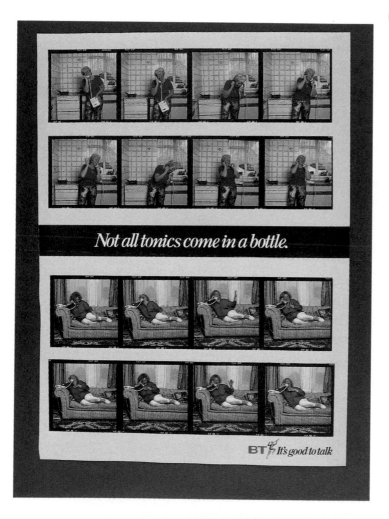

Not all tonics come in a bottle.

BT It's good to talk

What can you see in the picture?

Look at what is shown in the picture.

- What sort of people are they? Try to describe their clothes, age, facial expressions, body language, relationship to each other.
- What are they doing? How is this linked with the product?
- Where are they? Describe the background and what it suggests to you in as much detail as you can. What is the mood and atmosphere of the advert?
- What is the product being sold? Where does it appear in the advert?
- What can you tell about the product from all the visual information you have just studied?

What can you tell from the writing in the advert?

Look at all the written parts of the advert.

- What links are there between the words and the pictures?
- Do the words have any double meanings? Try to explain them and why you think they have been chosen.
- Is there a slogan linked with the product? How does it link with the pictures?
- What sort of writing style/typeface has been chosen? Can you think of any reasons for this?

How has the advert been put together?

Try to analyse what you can see.

- What colours have been used? Why do you think they have been chosen?
- Why do you think photographs have been used?
- Why are the photographs in a sequence? Why aren't there just two?

Now try to think about some of the technical details.

- What is the lighting in the advert like? Why?
- What kind of camera shots have been used? Why do you think this is?
- What is your eye drawn to in the pictures? What link do you think this has with the product being sold?

Who is this advert aimed at?

- What sort of person would respond to this sort of advert? How can you tell?
- Where do you think you would find this sort of advert? Why do you think this?

Who has made the advert? What does it represent?

- Is this advert part of a larger campaign? How do you know?
- What are the advert's overall messages?
- What sort of people are represented in the advert?
- What sort of lifestyles are associated with the advert?

Activity

Try making up your own advert.

1 Choose your product – it could be an item of food, a drink, a business or company, a CD, a magazine, etc.
2 It would be helpful to research a selection of advertisements for your chosen type of product:
   - see how many different types of advert you can find and choose the one that you think is the most successful
   - ask yourself some of the questions listed above before you choose a design for your own advert
3 When you are planning your advert, write down a detailed explanation of what you want it to show and why. Using the headings from this unit to help you, make sure you include the following information:
   - why you have chosen your particular setting (people, colours, mood, etc.)
   - what you can tell from the writing in your advert
   - what you have tried to make the main focus and how you have tried to do this
   - who your advert is aimed at

Follow-up

- For more help on reading for detail, see pages 44–45.
- For more help on reading for meaning, see pages 46–47.

Media Texts

Media

Information in our society is communicated to us in a variety of ways – through newspapers, magazines, television, radio, cinema, pictures, posters, etc. Such means of communication might be visual, aural, printed, taped, or a combination of all of these.

Activity

1 Look at the media samples on page 58. When trying to understand the sort of information they are conveying, it can be helpful to ask yourself a number of questions. Try and answer the questions for each of the different media samples that are shown, writing down your answers.
   - **Who?** Who has produced it?
   - **What?** What is it about?
   - **Where?** Where is it aimed? (Who is the audience?)
   - **When?** When was it made?
   - **Why?** Why was it made?

2 Now try to analyse how and reflect on why you have responded to the media samples in the way that you have. Look at your reactions both to the nature of the information and the style of its presentation.

Activity

Look at the extract below in which a scientist, called Frankenstein, has just discovered the secret of life. Using all the information, and bringing the language up-to-date, try and write the following:

- a dialogue in the form of an interview between the scientist and a TV presenter – the TV interviewer wants to know all about what it is that Frankenstein has discovered and is doing
- a sensational newspaper article aimed at an audience which likes thrills and scares
- a factual television news report

Frankenstein

After days and nights of incredible labour and fatigue, I succeeded in discovering the cause and generation of life; nay, more, I became myself capable of bestowing animation upon lifeless matter ... What had been the study and desire of the wisest men since the creation of the world, was now within my grasp ...

When I found so astonishing a power placed within my hands, I hesitated a long time concerning the manner in which I should employ it. Although I possessed the capacity of bestowing animation, yet to prepare a frame for the reception of it, with all its intricacies of fibres, muscles, veins, still remained a work of inconceivable difficulty and labour. I doubted at first whether I should attempt the creation of a being like myself ... but ... I began the creation of an human being.

Mary Shelley

Follow-up

- For help on ways of presenting speech, see pages 40–41.
- For help on writing dialogue, see pages 80–81.
- For help on interviewing, see page 39.
- For help on writing a report, see pages 70–71.

Assignment: Comprehension

Postcards

Liz and Chris have spent the last two weeks travelling around France. Work out their route by reading the postcards on these two pages and following the map. Then write up the appropriate diary entries for each day, inventing more details about the holiday. (Before you start, look at the follow-up suggestions on page 61.) Liz and Chris plan to be back in London on Sunday night, as they have to get home in time for work on Monday morning. What time train would you advise them to get in Paris?

Postcard 1

Tues 12th, Cancale

Made it to France yesterday via Guernsey after a calm crossing. What a wonderful spot Cancale is – cliff-top walks, non-stop sea-food, and super views over the sea-front. We plan to stay here for a couple of days so we can sample the local oysters and take a trip to Mont St Michel before we move south to Tours.

Regards Liz and Chris

Postcard 2

Heading south to the sun!   17. 7. 94
I'm amazed we've already been here for a day. It was a relief to get away from Tours – fancy arriving there on Bastille Day! What idiots! Still the chateaux of the Loire were well worth seeing and it was worth putting up with all the crowds. We're well away from them now and are enjoying a sample of the local wine. Heading for the Spanish border tomorrow. If we've time we might even pop into Spain.

Love L & C

Tony Baxter
182 Christchurch
London SW15

Postcard 3

Thursday

We'll need a holiday after this – the 5th place we've visited! It's a pity we've only got two nights here, because this city certainly comes alive after dark – plenty of superb restaurants and lively night-clubs. Mustn't overdo it and miss the early morning flight to Paris on Saturday!

See you soon, Liz & Chris

Postcard 4

Our last day!

Heaps to see here. We had a trip along the Seine and went up the Eiffel Tower yesterday and hope to fit in the Pompidou Centre before getting on the train for home. I can't wait to sample the Channel Tunnel!

Liz & Chris.

July

11 Monday	
12 Tuesday	19 Tuesday
13 Wednesday	20 Wednesday
14 Thursday	21 Thursday
15 Friday	22 Friday
16 Saturday	23 Saturday
17 Sunday	24 Sunday

SUNDAY SERVICE

Paris ➤ London	
Paris Nord	London Waterloo
13.07	15.30
15.19	17.13
16.07	18.13
17.10	19.13
17.46	19.43
18.18	20.13
19.19	21.13
20.07	22.13

Follow-up
- For help on reading techniques, see pages 42–47.
- For help on maps and charts, see pages 54–55.
- For help on writing diary entries, see pages 50–51.

Planning and Drafting

Objectives:

- to be able to organize ideas and plan them into paragraphs
- to draft and perfect a piece of writing

Clear and Effective Writing

Some careful thought and planning before you write a final version of a piece of work will make your writing much more clear and effective. Without planning and drafting, pieces of writing can be rambling and without shape.

In writing about a particular subject the following steps should help you.

Stage One – Thinking

Before you begin to write you should think about and decide on some of the following things:

- What are you writing about? What is your *topic*?
- Are you likely to need information?
- What kind of writing is it going to be? What is the *form*?
  poetry? narrative? informative? descriptive? persuasive?
  letter? playscript?
- Who are you writing it for? Who is your *audience*? What are they likely to know already about the topic?
- Why are you writing? What is your *purpose*?
  to entertain? to amuse? to inform? to persuade? to excite?

Stage Two – Notes

If, for example, you decided that you were going to write an essay to inform your friends and teacher about the ways we live with animals in our world, you would need to write down all your ideas in note form, perhaps in a topic web:

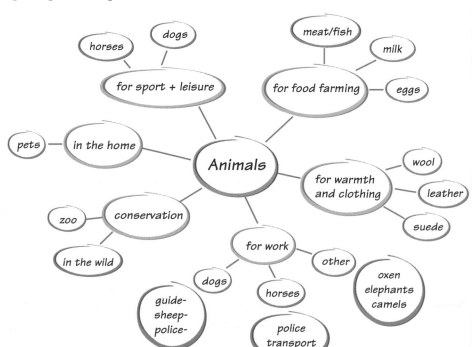

Stage Three – Outline

Once you have jotted down all the ideas you can think of, you need to organize them into some sort of shape or plan. You could use a word processor from this point. If you used a topic web, you will see how some points become topics for paragraphs in their own right, and others will combine to form a paragraph. You will often see that several ideas can be linked together and these start to form the outline of how you are going to organize your paragraphs.

Note: If some ideas seem short of details, you could carry out a bit of research at this stage, e.g. finding out how camels are used for transport in the Middle East.

First paragraph
General introduction mentioning how much we depend on animals in all sorts of different ways

Second paragraph
How we use animals:
• for food and in farming
• for warmth and clothing
• for work

Third paragraph
How animals are part of sport and leisure activities

Fourth paragraph
Animals in the home:
• pets

Fifth paragraph
The importance of conservation:
• in the wild
• zoos

Stage Four – First Draft

Check that your ideas are grouped together sensibly and that they make sense. You may need to reorder some ideas within your paragraphs and/or rephrase some of them. Now write up your notes in carefully arranged paragraphs. You may need to add or take away information at this stage.

Stage Five – Final Copy

When you are happy with the organization of your first draft, the next step is to make sure that spellings and punctuation are accurate. Then write up your final copy.

Note: The process just described can be used for many of the writing activities in Section 4.

Activity

Using the five stages outlined above, plan, draft, and write an essay of approximately five paragraphs on a topic of your choice. If you are short of ideas, choose from the following: fire, water, wood, pollution.

Follow-up
• For help on making notes, see page 48.
• For help on organizing paragraphs, see pages 20–21.
• For more on planning and drafting, see the following unit.

Argumentative Writing

Using Connectives

An argumentative essay is a piece of writing in which you put across your views and opinions. You have to step back from the issues and attempt to give both sides of an argument in a balanced and objective way. To do this effectively you need to be able to plan paragraphs carefully and use a variety of *connective* words appropriately. These help to lead an argument along in a structured and logical way.

In other words That is to say	But Still However Yet Meanwhile Nevertheless On the other hand On the contrary In spite of this	To begin with In the first place Firstly Secondly Lastly Finally	Moreover Furthermore What is more In addition … also … Nor	Naturally Of course Certainly Oddly enough Luckily Fortunately Unfortunately Admittedly Undoubtedly	As a result Consequently So Therefore Thus Accordingly
Finally In conclusion In short To sum up		**CONNECTIVES**			
Next Later Eventually		For this reason Owing to this … therefore …	In comparison In contrast Similarly		For example For instance Thus

Planning your Arguments

In drafting an argumentative essay, you need to assemble your ideas.

1 Gather all the arguments in favour of the topic and arrange them in separate columns or in a topic web.
2 Then assemble all the arguments you can think of against the topic.

For example, if you had to write an essay on film editing/censorship for TV screening you might begin your topic web like this.

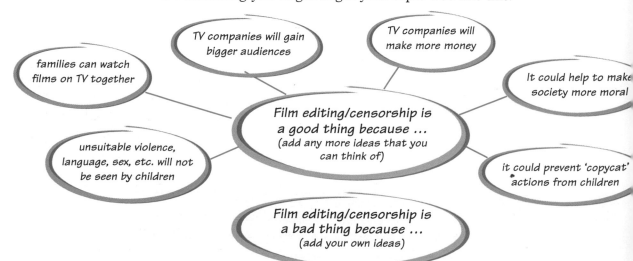

families can watch films on TV together

TV companies will gain bigger audiences

TV companies will make more money

It could help to make society more moral

Film editing/censorship is a good thing because … (add any more ideas that you can think of)

unsuitable violence, language, sex, etc. will not be seen by children

it could prevent 'copycat' actions from children

Film editing/censorship is a bad thing because … (add your own ideas)

Once you have assembled your ideas, try to follow these steps.

- Aim for a general introduction which will outline the scope of your essay.
- Draft linked paragraphs in favour of the topic.
- Draft linked paragraphs against the topic.
- Use appropriate connective words.
- Write a concluding paragraph where your own view becomes clear.
- Make the final essay between 400 and 500 words long.

The first draft below is the start of an essay written by a 14-year-old boy. Do you think he has followed the steps outlined above? Can you improve on what he has written?

First Draft

Films that are shown on television are often edited to be made suitable for family audiences, or to allow television companies to show them early in the evening or day. However, the editing does not please all television watchers, and many have strong views on the subject. The possible reasons for and against film editing are now quite big issues that often appear in newspapers and on television, so, as more and more modern films are brought to our television screens, the arguments become more and more common to read and hear about.

Firstly, the reasons for television film editing are quite responsible, as they could be seen as a way of making our society a better one. Many films are considered to be unsuitable for children, but by taming them down, they are made otherwise. So by doing this, more parents would allow their children to watch these films, and so television companies would have a wider audience for them.

Thoughts about the draft

I'm trying to start in a general way to put my reader in the picture and I'm trying to keep my tone formal and impersonal.

I need to set up the two sides before going into details.

'However' tells my reader that a change is coming along.

Am I writing clearly and relevantly?

I should include an example so it doesn't get too general.

I need to develop each main idea in a paragraph of its own.

Activity

1 Redraft the part of the essay above and continue it with more ideas in support of the argument, followed by ideas about the disadvantages. Then add your own conclusion.

2 Write your own essay, using your own topic or one of the following:
   pocket money   animal-rights   smoking   arming the police
   You don't need to put both sides of the argument equally every time. You might choose to argue in favour of one side and only briefly mention the opposition arguments in order to say why you don't agree with them.

Follow-up
- For more on the use of objectivity, see page 47.
- For more help on planning and drafting, see pages 62–63.
- For more help on writing persuasively, see the following unit.

Persuasive Forms and Techniques

- to learn more about how persuasive techniques work
- to develop your own powers of persuasive writing

Language to Influence and Persuade

Using language to influence and persuade is a way of getting others to do or believe what you want them to. Perhaps advertising is the form of persuasion that you are most familiar with, but there are other techniques too.

In Shakespeare's play *Henry V*, England and France are at war. The English army has crossed over into France and is camped outside the town of Harfleur. It is the eve of the battle of Agincourt and the English king, Harry, is trying to raise the spirits of his soldiers and persuade them that they are the very best.

King Harry: Once more unto the breach, dear friends, once more,
Or close the wall up with our English dead.
… And you, good yeomen,
Whose limbs were made in England, show us here
The mettle of your pasture; let us swear
That you are worth your breeding – which I doubt not,
For there is none of you so mean and base
That hath not noble lustre in your eyes.
I see you stand like greyhounds in the slips,
Straining upon the start. The game's afoot.
Follow your spirit, and upon this charge
Cry, 'God for Harry! England and Saint George!'

Activity   How many of the persuasive 'tricks' listed below can you find in King Harry's speech? (You might need to look up some of the terms in the glossary at the back of this book.)
- involving the listeners and speaking personally to them
- appealing to the emotions
- using alliteration
- repeating for emphasis
- using the rule of three
- using rhetorical techniques
- ending strongly

I Protest!

Imagine that a new law has just been passed:

> By 8 p.m. all people of 14 and under
> must be at home and in bed!

From the New Year, the government will require all young people to go to bed early. They feel that this new law will have dual benefits: it will cut crime figures and, by increasing concentration and alertness in school, will raise academic standards. You are so annoyed by this new law that you feel you must make a protest.

Activity   1 Write a letter either to a newspaper or to your MP asking for some support in your efforts to get this law changed. You will need to think carefully about the sort of letter to write and the tone of voice to use if you want people to take you seriously. State all the facts and try to demonstrate how absurd the law is.

2 You decide to call a meeting for all young people who feel similarly outraged. Design a poster to draw attention to your campaign and to give details of the meeting. The style of the poster must appeal to young people. Make sure you include all the vital information, but at the same time try to keep your poster simple and eye-catching. Try to include a memorable and effective slogan.

3 Write a speech that you could make to encourage your supporters. Choose your words with care and develop your ideas clearly. You must try to persuade your listeners that you should all join together to protest and you should try to make them feel excited and enthusiastic.

Note: Use the techniques detailed on the previous page and in the previous unit to help you.

Follow-up
- For more information on letter-writing, see pages 72–73.
- For help on designing an advert, see pages 56–57.
- For more help on making and writing a speech, see pages 36–37.

Describing Processes

- to learn more about practical writing
- to develop your ability to write clearly and logically

Writing Instructions

When the poet Sir John Betjeman was asked for his favourite recipe for the benefit of young readers, he offered a recipe for boiling an egg. Perhaps he was more used to writing poetry, or perhaps he did not know much about cooking – what do you think?

All I know about cooking is how to boil an egg, and I can give you a recipe for this. Take a saucepan and fill it with water, warm if possible so that it does not take quite so long to come to the boil as it would if it were cold. Now get an egg, preferably a fresh one, and put it into the water, at the same time trying to avoid scalding your fingers. I forgot to say that the water must be boiling before you insert the egg. One way I have found of putting in the egg without burning my fingers and cracking the shell is to put it in with a spoon. Leave it in the boiling water for a few minutes. You can never tell whether it's going to be too soft or hard. That is one of the many mysteries of cooking.

John Betjeman

If you had never boiled an egg before and really needed to know how to go about it, perhaps a different style of writing would have been more useful!

When describing how something is done or how something is made, it is important to think about the following:

- who you are writing for
- whether your language is clear and easy to understand
- avoiding words that explain your feelings and opinions
  e.g. lovely, horrible, disgusting
- giving instructions in the form of imperatives (commands)
  e.g. 'take a pan', 'get an egg', etc.
- whether the information is in the right order
- whether a reader can follow what to do, step by step
- whether to use numbered paragraphs, illustrations, or diagrams

Activity   Rewrite the instructions for boiling an egg for a young person who has had no experience of cooking. Present your instructions as clearly and precisely as you can.

Charting Information

A different way of presenting instructions and information can be in the form of a chart:

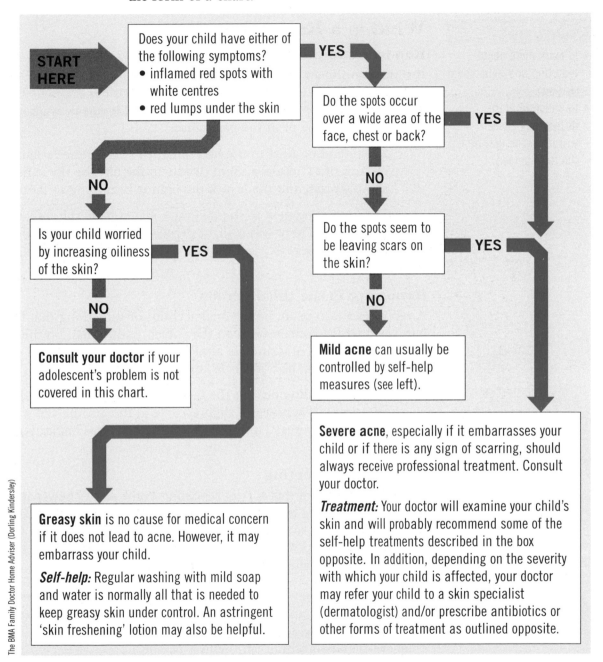

START HERE

Does your child have either of the following symptoms?
• inflamed red spots with white centres
• red lumps under the skin

YES

Do the spots occur over a wide area of the face, chest or back?

YES

NO

NO

Is your child worried by increasing oiliness of the skin?

YES

Do the spots seem to be leaving scars on the skin?

YES

NO

NO

Consult your doctor if your adolescent's problem is not covered in this chart.

Mild acne can usually be controlled by self-help measures (see left).

Severe acne, especially if it embarrasses your child or if there is any sign of scarring, should always receive professional treatment. Consult your doctor.

Treatment: Your doctor will examine your child's skin and will probably recommend some of the self-help treatments described in the box opposite. In addition, depending on the severity with which your child is affected, your doctor may refer your child to a skin specialist (dermatologist) and/or prescribe antibiotics or other forms of treatment as outlined opposite.

Greasy skin is no cause for medical concern if it does not lead to acne. However, it may embarrass your child.

Self-help: Regular washing with mild soap and water is normally all that is needed to keep greasy skin under control. An astringent 'skin freshening' lotion may also be helpful.

The BMA Family Doctor Home Adviser (Dorling Kindersley)

Activity
1 Try rewriting the chart as a series of numbered points.
2 Then extend it into a continuous piece of writing. Remember that connectives are very useful in this sort of writing.

Which way of presenting instructions do you find the easiest to follow?

Follow-up
• For help on using connectives, see page 64.

Reporting

Objectives:

- to learn more about reporting and impersonal writing
- to understand the difference between writing in the first and the third person

What is a Report?

Reporting in the first person

A report can be an eye-witness account where a person describes clearly and accurately what is happening or what has happened. This is called writing in the first person (using 'I') and it can be written either in the present tense or in the past tense.

> I am standing next to the taxi rank just outside the Italian restaurant. There is a slight drizzle in the air, the sky is heavy and overcast, and the last of the light is beginning to fade.

> I was standing next to the taxi rank just outside the Italian restaurant. There was a slight drizzle in the air, the sky was heavy and overcast, and the last of the light was beginning to fade.

Reporting in the third person

A report can also be an impersonal account of something that has happened which concentrates on the subject rather than on the reporter. This sort of writing is always in the past tense and in the third person (using 'he', 'she', 'it', or 'they').

> He was standing next to the taxi rank just outside the Italian restaurant. There was a slight drizzle in the air, the sky was heavy and overcast, and the last of the light was beginning to fade.

Newspaper reporting

You see examples of this sort of reporting every day. A newspaper report tries to bring an event to life for a reader, often playing on a reader's emotions, so it is easy to imagine what has happened. Certain techniques are used to tempt you to read further and to make sure that all the important information is mentioned first.

Activity

Look at the sketch and the reporter's notes on page 71 and then write two accounts of the accident:

- an eye-witness account (in the first person)
- a newspaper report (in the third person)

You will need to add some information of your own. Then organize your ideas for each account into three paragraphs:

> **paragraph 1** should introduce the bare facts of the incident
> **paragraph 2** should give a little more information, such as names and addresses
> **paragraph 3** should develop the information further, so that all the important points have been covered

Reporter's notes

Man – 82 yrs – (name?) (address?) – knocked down – car – (reactions of driver?) – crossing from Hog's Head Pub to small market – driver braked hard – not speeding – visibility poor – dusk, drizzle and overcast – (severity of accident?) (police?) (human interest angle on old man?)

This example of a news report may help with your writing.

TEENAGER IN HORROR FALL

A schoolboy is lucky to be alive after plummeting from a roof onto a school building skylight.

The 14-year-old, who has not been named, said he was trying to find his tennis ball which had been hit onto the school roof, when he slipped and fell.

His fall was broken when he crashed onto a perspex skylight of a building eight feet below. Stunned friends called for help, and fire crews and paramedics stretchered the boy down. He was given oxygen treatment and rushed to hospital with neck injuries and severe cuts to his left leg.

Working on

Use the news report 'Teenager in Horror Fall', and try to rewrite it as a story from the point of view of the 14-year-old boy and his friends. You can write either in the first person or the third person and you should include some direct speech and descriptive detail to make it as interesting as you can. Do you think he had really gone to find his tennis ball, or were he and his friends up to no good?

Follow-up
- For more help on note-making, see page 48.
- For more help on planning and drafting, see pages 62–63.

Writing Letters

Formal Letters

There are many situations where you need to be able to write formal letters in such a way that what you are saying will be noticed – perhaps in applying for a job, or to express what you feel about something important, or to make arrangements with officials and organizations.

There are certain rules about how these letters should be written:
• they should be written in Standard English
• they are set out in a certain way
• they should contain sensible and serious ideas

Most word-processed formal letters are fully blocked, not traditionally set out. Commas and full stops are only used in the main part of the letter.

Include the name and address of who you are writing to.

Date usually comes under this address.

Write person's name if you know it.

Use block paragraphs rather than indenting.

Leave a line between paragraphs.

Only the first word begins with a capital. If you know the name of the person you're writing to, end with 'Yours sincerely'.

Sign your name formally.

Print your name below your signature.

21 Oak Way
Horley
Surrey
RH11 2PX

The Manager
School's Bus Service
Industrial Estate
CRAWLEY
Sussex

24 January 1994

Dear Sir

I am writing to complain about your buses. I have been back at school for three days now, after the Christmas holidays, and on each of these three days your buses have been over half an hour late, leaving me in the freezing cold. This has also got me into trouble at school for being late.

I was wondering if there was anything you could do to make your service more efficient and reliable, as it is a long journey from Horley to my school in Crawley every day.

Yours faithfully

A. Brown

A Brown (Miss)

Activity   Write the bus company's reply to this letter, using a similar formal layout.

Informal Letters

When you are writing informal letters, you have much more freedom in the tone and style of writing you choose, and you do not need to include the name and address of the person you are writing to.

Traditional layout slopes.

Use punctuation.

No punctuation.

Leave a margin and end the greeting with a comma.

Indent and start with a capital letter.

Use a capital for the first word of the ending and a comma at the end of it.

Date starts under house number.

If you're writing to a friend use your first name.

21 Oak Way,
Horley,
Surrey.
RH11 2PX

Tuesday, 10th April

Dear Julie,

Many thanks for inviting us to your party. Chris and I would love to come. Looking forward to seeing you on Saturday.

Love,
Angela

In Anne Fine's book *A Pack of Liars*, Laura reads the most boring letter she has ever read:

2D Cathedral Close
Sticklebury

Dear Friend
Would you like to write to me? I would like that. It would be nice. I hope you will. How are you? I hope you are well... Where do you live? Are there lots of houses on your street? There are a lot of houses on my street. What is your house like? How many rooms do you have? Do you have lots of neighbours like we do?... Do you have any pets? I have no pets. Do you have a colour television? We do. Do you have a video?

We do. Ours is new. Is yours new? We have four radio-cassette players in our house. How many do you have? We have a stereo system, too. Do you have a stereo system? We have a computer. Do you have a computer? What sort is it? We have some electric hedge shears. Do you have any electric hedge shears? We keep ours in the garden shed. Where do you keep yours? We have a microwave oven. Do you?

With best wishes,
Your penpal,
Philip

Activity Write a tactful reply to Philip's letter, in which you try to find out more about him. At the same time try to give information about yourself in an interesting way.

Follow-up • For help on Standard English, see page 30.

Writing to Publicize

Objectives:

- to learn more about different forms of publicity
- to experiment with publicity forms of your own

Publicity Material

Publicity material comes in a variety of forms (leaflets, pamphlets, advertisements, etc.) and covers a great range of topics. It can:
- provide the public with information
- inform us about potential dangers in life
- give information about products
- try to attract us to places of interest
- advertise all of these ideas

To get its message across, publicity material has to be bright and attractive or nobody will bother to read it. At the same time the information has to be clear, to the point, and easy to understand.

Look at the following leaflet advertising Hastings:

Note how the headings give a flavour of the past.

The language is persuasive. Layout is attractive, with small sections of text broken up by illustration.

Illustrations are vivid and exciting.

 Activity   Using the Hastings leaflet as a model, design your own leaflet. Before you start:
- choose a topic of your own
  e.g. a place of local interest   your school   keeping a pet
- gather together all the information that you might need
- decide who your target audience will be

Using Humour

The instructions below are aimed at helping young people live safely in their homes. Even though the ideas being communicated are serious and important, the use of humour, especially in the illustrations, helps to make the message more persuasive.

Guide to Safety in the Home

NEVER
STICK ANYTHING INTO AN ELECTRICAL SOCKET EXCEPT A PLUG.
You could get a nasty electrical shock.

You could have an accident if you balance on chairs, tables, or anything else to try to reach something just beyond your grasp.

WAIT
FOR SOMEONE TALLER TO HELP YOU.

MAKE SURE YOU KNOW WHAT YOU ARE EATING OR DRINKING **BEFORE** YOU PUT IT IN YOUR MOUTH.

Some things might look nice to eat but they could be dangerous.

Activity

1 What is the difference between this sort of humorous approach compared to a set of rules or DOs and DON'Ts? How can you tell that it is aimed at young people?

2 Make a list of DOs and DON'Ts about a particular subject, for example Safety in the Water. You will need to decide who your audience will be before you begin.

3 Now design a safety leaflet on the same subject but this time see if you can add a touch of humour so that it might appeal more to the audience you have in mind. Include some illustrations if you would like.

Follow-up
- For help on using persuasive language, see pages 66–67.
- For help on using fact and opinion, see pages 46–47.
- For more on advertising, see pages 56–57.

Imaginative Writing

Channelling the Imagination

When you are using your imagination in writing, e.g. writing in character as a response to a class novel, you need to look at things in a new way and try to make your readers see and feel what you are describing. Do not tell them what to feel, make them feel it!

Activity Experiment with expanding this sentence into a much more powerful piece of writing. You should end up with a short paragraph.

Try to describe how dusk is falling.

What can you see? What can you feel?

As it got dark, it started to get windy and I could see there was going to be a storm. I was frightened.

How do you know? What can you see?

What do you feel? Are your hands sweaty? Are you breathing more deeply? Describe your feelings.

Getting Started

If you have to write something longer, a little planning will help you a lot. Asking yourself the following questions will provide a good framework for your writing.

Where?

You need to think about where your piece of writing will take place, and build up descriptions that are in keeping with this setting or place.

When?

You will need to decide if your writing is going to take place in the past, the present, or the future. Decide whether you are going to write about, for example:
- one particular moment – a snapshot in time
- a sequence of events through the course of a day
- a particular season, or a contrast between seasons

Who?

You need to think about who you are writing *for*:
- younger readers
- older readers
- people of your own age

You also need to decide who you are going to write *about*:
- what do they look like?
- what kind of people are they?
- why are they there?
- what are they doing?

Why?

You will need to give some thought to why you are writing. For example:

- to influence and make a point about something serious
- to give information
- as a bit of fun – for pleasure
- to provide excitement or mystery

What?

You also need to think about what the overall piece of writing is going to be about – what is going to happen? Is it one of the following:

- an adventure?
- a news item?
- science fiction?

How?

Decide how you are going to organize your writing. You could write:

- in the first person – as if it is happening to you
- in the third person – as if you are repeating information
- as a narrator – as if you know what is going on in everyone's mind

Think too about the shape your writing will have – how it will begin, develop, and end.

Using the Five Senses

Another way of helping your reader share what you are trying to describe is to use as many of the five senses as are appropriate.

Sight	Describe in detail what you can see.
Sound	What sounds are there?
Touch	Are there any textures you can describe more precisely?
Smell	This could be either pleasant or unpleasant.
Taste	Often, but not always, linked with smell.

Working on

Using as many of these ideas as you can, write a first draft of 300 words on the following title: The Bonfire. Aim to produce a story or description that could be included in a school magazine, to be read by the school community and parents.

Now look at your writing again. Are there any sections you could expand or change to encourage your readers to share what you are writing about? Experiment with several changes until you are ready to write a final copy.

Follow-up

- For more help on planning and drafting, see pages 62–63.
- For help on narrative techniques, see pages 92–93.

Personal and Reflective Writing

Memories

Personal and reflective writing draws on your own experiences and feelings. Diaries, journals, and autobiographies are all examples of this sort of writing, where people reflect on their early memories, describing people, places, feelings, emotions, and experiences. In the following extracts from his novel *Paddy Clarke Ha Ha Ha*, you can see how Roddy Doyle uses these techniques rather than using a fictional character.

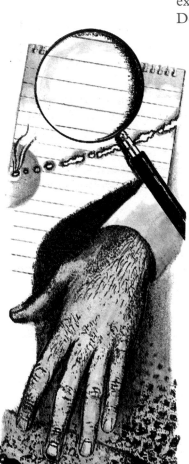

What You Used to Do

I preferred magnifying glasses to matches. We spent afternoons burning little piles of cut grass. I loved watching the grass change colour. I loved it when the flame used to race through the grass. You had more control with a magnifying glass. It was easier but it took more skill. If the sun stayed out long enough you could saw through a sheet of paper and not have to touch it, just put down a stone in each corner to stop it from blowing away. We'd have a race; burn, blow it out, burn, blow it out. Last to burn the paper completely in half had to let the other fella burn his hand.

People You Knew

My da's hands were big. The fingers were long. They weren't fat. I could make out the bone under the skin and the flesh. He had one of his hands dangling over the chair. He was holding his book with his other hand. His nails were clean – except for one – and the white bits at the top were longer than mine. The wrinkles at his knuckles were a bit like the design of a wall, the cement between the bricks up and across. There weren't many other wrinkles but the pores were like hollows, with a hair for every pore. Dark hair. Hair came out from under his cuff.

Places You Knew

The roads were cement, all the roads round our way, the parts that hadn't been dug up. The roads were cement and the tar went between the slabs of cement. It was hard and you didn't notice it for most of the time but when it softened and bubbled it was great. The top was old and grey looking, like an elephant's skin around its eyes, but under that, when you got your ice-pop stick in, there was new tar, black and soft, a bit like toffee that had been in your mouth. You burst the bubble and the clean soft tar was under there; the top was gone off the bubble – it was a volcano. Pebbles went in; they died screaming.

Your Experiences

An earwig flew into my mouth once. I was charging, it was in front of me – then gone. There was a taste, that was all. I swallowed. It was far back, too far to cough out. My eyes went watery but I wasn't crying. It was in the school yard. There was still a horrible taste. Like petrol. I went to the toilet and got my head under the tap. I drank for ages. I wanted the taste to go and I wanted to drown the earwig. It had gone down whole. Straight down.

Roddy Doyle

Activity

1 Write four paragraphs of your own, similar to the ones above, but using your own memories and experiences. Because you are drawing on actual memories, the details should be more vivid and convincing than ones you make up.

As with any other sort of writing, you need to plan and shape your ideas otherwise you may end up with a rather jumbled list. You also need to select details that will catch and hold your reader's attention.

2 Look at the plan and first draft below of a piece of writing about an embarrassing moment. Redraft the writing into something which stands out and attracts your attention. Use the notes around the text to help you.

Plan

- The situation: shopping with parents and older sister.
- What happened next: falling into a window display, making apologies.
- Reflections: embarrassment, pain, then being able to see the funny side of it – no ill effects.

Describe the background to make the writing realistic.

First draft

We need to picture these characters through actions, words, thoughts, and reactions.

An Embarrassing Moment
When I was ten I went Christmas shopping with my mum, dad, and sister. We had been in the shops for about two hours. I was getting really tired. I asked if we could go home but my mum said we had to go into one more shop. We were deciding to go home or not. I had a dizzy spell so I wanted to lean on something so I saw a window display so I went over to lean on it but I didn't realize that there wasn't any glass on the front. I fell right into it and a shop assistant came running over. I was so embarrassed. I looked up and saw my mum, dad, and sister laughing. I got a bit upset and ran out the shop and started to cry. I felt hurt and really embarrassed. It wasn't funny at the time but it is now.

Add speech?

What happened to the display?

Describe bodily reactions and include dialogue.

Follow-up

- For more help on planning and drafting, see pages 62–63.
- For more help on imaginative writing, see pages 76–77.

Writing Dialogue

Dialogue Rules

When you are using dialogue in a passage of writing, there are only three main rules to remember:

1 The words that are spoken must be placed inside inverted commas.
2 The dialogue must be separated from the rest of the writing by a comma, full stop, question mark, or exclamation mark.
3 Each time there is a different speaker, you must begin a new paragraph.

Why We Use Dialogue in Stories

There are not any hard and fast rules for whether stories should contain dialogue or not but, on the whole, conversation helps in a number of ways:

- it breaks the writing up and makes a story easier to read
- it helps vary the pace of the text
- it involves readers more closely with what is going on
- characters and the situations they are in become much more lifelike and vivid
- it can emphasize the particular mood of a scene or incident – make it funnier, sadder, or more tense

Read the following extract and see how the dialogue brings the story to life.

Vet in a Spin

Farmer Hollin has a problem as the new-born piglets on his farm are being rejected by their mother, Gertrude. James Herriot, the vet, is trying out a new wonder drug which he is sure will solve the problem.

Gertrude popped out another pink, squirming piglet. The farmer leaned over, and gently nudged the little creature towards the udder as the sow lay on her side. As soon as the nose made contact with the teat the big pig was up in a flash, all growls and yellow teeth.

He snatched the piglet away quickly and deposited it with the others in a tall cardboard box …

'Well, she's cleaned herself,' Mr Hollin said gloomily. 'So it looks like she's finished. And now I've got fifteen pigs to rear without their mother's milk. I could lose all this lot.'

'Nay, nay,' a voice said from the open doorway. 'You won't lose 'em.' I looked round. It was Grandad Hollin, his face set in its customary smile. He marched to the pen and poked Gertrude's ribs with his stick. She responded with a snarl, and the old man's smile grew broader …

'Why, she just wants quietin', tha knows.'

'Yes, Mr Hollin, that's exactly what I've been trying to do.'

'Aye, but you're not doin' it the right way, young man.'

… 'Well, I've given her the latest injection,' I mumbled.

He shook his head.

'She don't want injections, she wants beer … Right, ah'll slip down to the pub. Won't be long.'

… It was a relief when Grandad returned bearing an enamel bucket brimming with brown liquid.

'By gaw,' he chuckled. 'You should've seen their face down at t'Waggon and Horses. Reckon they've never heard of a two gallon order afore.'

I gaped at him.

'You've got two gallons of beer?'

… Grandad poised his bucket. He leaned over the rail, and sent a dark cascade frothing into the empty trough. Gertrude ambled moodily across, and sniffed at the strange fluid. After some hesitation, she dipped her snout and tried a tentative swallow, and within seconds the building echoed with a busy slobbering.

'By heck, she likes it!' Will exclaimed …

It took the big sow a surprisingly short time to consume the two gallons, and when she had finished, she licked out every corner of the trough before turning away … Gertrude was stoned to the wide … The old man gestured towards the cardboard box.

'Put the little 'uns in now,' he said …

Fifteen ravenous little mouths fastened on to the teats …

James Herriot

Activity

1 Use dialogue to carry on with the story at the farm.
2 Then write the conversation at the surgery, as the vet tells his partners about the incident.

Try to be aware of the following points:
- Think about and describe a natural and convincing background.
- Make your characters interesting and 'real'.
- Make sure the spoken words you use are appropriate to the people speaking them and to the situation they are in.
- Do not use too much speech.
- Try not to overuse the word 'said'. Try consciously to use a variety of synonyms such as: asked, murmured, demanded, etc.
- Remember that it is sometimes more effective not to use 'he said', etc., at all, leaving the speech to stand alone.

Follow-up • For more on presenting speech, see pages 40–41.

Poetry Writing

Objectives:

- to become familiar with some different poetic forms
- to develop skills in writing poetry

What is a Poem?

A group of words in a pattern?

Lines that rhyme?

A sort of story?

Whatever you want it to be?

Something that shows a poet's feelings?

You might feel that a poem is some or all of these things depending on what sort of poem you want to write. Poems come in all shapes and forms, without rhymes as free verse, with rhymes and in verses, following set shapes or syllable patterns.

Rhyming Verse

Silver

Slowly, silently, now the moon
Walks the night in her silver shoon;
This way, and that, she peers, and sees
Silver fruit upon silver trees;
One by one the casements catch
Her beams among the silvery thatch;
Couched in his kennel, like a log,
With paws of silver sleeps the dog;
From their shadowy cote the white breasts peep
Of doves in a silver-feathered sleep;
A harvest mouse goes scampering by,
With silver claws, and silver eye;
And moveless fish in the water gleam,
By silver reeds in a silver stream.

Walter de la Mare

Haiku

The snow blankets all
Transforming to still beauty,
Dazzling purity.

(Three lines with 17 syllables in all: 5, 7, 5)

List Poem

What is White?

White is a dove
And lily of the valley
And a puddle of milk
Spilled in an alley
A ship's sail
A kite's tail
A wedding veil
Hailstones and
Halibut bones
And some people's
Telephones.
The hottest and most blinding light
Is white …

Mary O'Neill

Free Verse

Our street is dead lazy
especially in winter.
Some mornings you wake up
and it's still lying there
saying nothing. Huddled
under its white counterpane.

Roger McGough

Drafting Poetry

Drafting is especially important when you are writing your own poems. It can take a lot of thinking and changing to get the best choice of words and shape or form of poem for what you want to say. Compare these first and final drafts of the same poem:

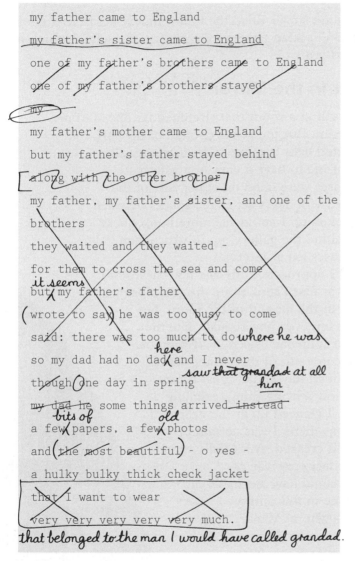

My Father's Father

my father came to England
my father's mother came to England
but my father's father stayed behind

so my dad had no dad here
and I never saw him at all

One day in Spring
some things arrived:
a few old papers, a few old photos
and – O yes –
a hulky bulky thick check jacket
that belonged to the man
I would have called Grandad.
The man who stayed behind.

But I kept the jacket
and I wore it and wore it and wore it,
till it wore right through at the back.

Michael Rosen

Activity Now try writing your own poem, using the following steps.

1 Choose your subject: memories, family, something you care about, etc.
2 Brainstorm on your subject, writing down words and phrases.
3 Arrange your words and phrases in various combinations.
4 Choose the form of poem that suits your ideas (free verse, haiku, rhyming verse, list poem, etc.) and write a first draft.
5 Work on this draft until you feel you can produce a final copy.

Follow-up
• For a limerick example, see page 6.
• For help writing diamantes, see page 9.

Assignment: Extended Writing

Objectives:

- to experiment with different forms of creative writing
- to recap on what you have learnt in this unit

Ghost Story

What makes a good story? Read the following extract from a ghost story. It is set in Victorian times in the library of a school which is two or three hundred years old.

The Mist in the Mirror

Hints about weather and time of day.

Detailed description of the library.

The ghostly happenings build up slowly.

Short sentences increase the tension.

Careful choice of words to emphasize mood and character.

Speech to break silence and tension, if only for a moment.

I found myself in a room that stretched far ahead of me into the gloom. But there was enough of the soft, snow-reflected light coming in through the tall windows for me to have a view of a gallery … Oak bookcases were lined on either side of the central aisle, with desks set in the spaces between, and as I looked up I could see more book stacks that rose behind the gallery, up to which iron spiral staircases led at intervals …

It was as I approached the last few bays that I heard what at first I took to be the soft closing of the door at the far end of the room, but which went on, even and regular, like the breathing of someone asleep, a sighing that seemed to come out of the air above my head, as though the whole, great room were somehow a living thing, exhaling around me. I glanced up at the gallery. Someone was there, I was certain of it. The wood creaked. A footfall. I was as far from my way of escape as I could have been, trapped alone in this empty place with – whom? What? …

The soft breathing came again from a different place, in the darkness just ahead of me, and I began to edge forwards, and then to stop, move and stop, but it was always just out of reach … Every shadow seemed like a crouched, huddled figure, every corner concealed some dreadful shape. There was no one there. There was nothing. There was everything.
'Who is there?' I said.
'What do you want of me? …'

I wanted to run but could not and knew that this was what was intended, that I should be terrified by nothing, by my own fears, by soft breathing, by the creak of a board, by the very atmosphere which threatened me …

The tension mounts. — And then I heard something else. It came from behind another door, an oak one set well back into the wall, with a

Careful descriptive — green curtain pulled half across, and partially concealing it.
detail.

I stood up close to it and waited, listened. It came again, faintly, from somewhere deep within, and was quite unmistakable. What I heard was a boy weeping …

Susan Hill

Activity

1 Imagine you are the person in the story who has heard the noises and the sobbing, and try to continue the story in the same style. Pay attention to descriptive detail, careful choice of words, mood, and atmosphere.

2 Write a letter to a friend explaining what has happened to you. Make sure you report accurately the details of the incident, as well as including your feelings and emotions.

3 Write the story down as it might appear in a newspaper under the headline:

GHOSTLY SOBS SPOOK SCHOOL VISITOR

Attempt to make the incident as sensational as you can.

4 Now try writing your own ghost story. You will need to think carefully about:
   • Who you are writing your story for – friends? a school magazine? a child?
   • What is going to happen in your story – you need a strong plot, which must be frightening but at the same time realistic.
   • Who the main characters are – you must try and make them into 'real' people, by including how old they are, what makes them different from each other, whether they have the same backgrounds/parents, how they speak, etc.
   • Where your story is set – should your characters be there at all or are they trespassing? Include detailed descriptions of the place and try to increase tension by giving details of the weather, the mood, the atmosphere. Using adjectives will help here.
   • How you will make your story frightening – will you describe the ghost, or just its noise, smell, or after-effects?

Follow-up
• For help on reporting, see pages 70–71.
• For help on writing letters, see pages 72–73.
• For help on imaginative writing, see pages 76–77.
• For help on setting and atmosphere, see pages 88–89.

Story, Plot, and Theme

Objectives:

- to consider story, plot, and genre
- to think about what themes are

Story and Plot

Stories have been with us for as long as humans have had language. We are surrounded by them in our everyday lives: on TV, films, and radio; in books, magazines, and newspapers. There are stories which are sad, funny, frightening, romantic, based on fantasy, space, folk-tales, and so on. These different types of story are often known as narrative genres.

When a story is written down and shaped into a narrative, an author is organizing and shaping the events. The outline of what happens in the story is usually known as the plot. A plot which is interesting and unexpected will tempt a reader to read on to see how problems and difficulties are going to be sorted out. Most plots follow a certain pattern:

1 Exposition	2 Complication	3 Climax	4 Resolution
This introduces the characters and the situation they are in.	Very soon a problem develops which disrupts their lives or changes things.	Matters are forced to a head,	and finally sorted out one way or another.

Activity

1 Choose a short and simple story that you know well and try to list the sequence of events that make up the plot.
2 Draw up your own chart like the one above and work out where the four stages of the plot occur.
3 Look at the opening of the story *Metamorphosis* by Franz Kafka (below). What do you think the climax of the story could be? How do you think it could end?
4 Continue the story, adding your own climax and resolution. How does he get out of bed? What happens when his mother tries to come in to wake him? What does he do?

Metamorphosis

As Gregor Samsa awoke one morning from uneasy dreams he found himself transformed in his bed into a gigantic insect. He was lying on his hard, as it were armour-plated back and when he lifted his head a little he could see his dome-like brown belly divided into stiff arched segments on top of which the bed-quilt could hardly keep in position and was about to slide off completely. His numerous legs, which were pitifully thin compared to the rest of his bulk, waved helplessly before his eyes.

What has happened to me? He thought. It was no dream. His room, a regular human bedroom, only rather too small, lay quiet between the four familiar walls …

Gregor's eyes turned next to the window, and the overcast sky – one could hear raindrops beating on the window gutter – made him quite melancholy. What about sleeping a little longer and forgetting all this nonsense, he thought, but it could not be done, for he was accustomed to sleep on his right side and in his present condition he could not turn himself over. However violently he forced himself towards his right side he always rolled on to his back again. He tried it at least a hundred times, shutting his eyes to keep from seeing his struggling legs …

Franz Kafka

Themes

While story and plot are concerned with sequences of events, themes are concerned with ideas. Most writers communicate certain ideas and beliefs through the telling of their stories. In the story of *Metamorphosis*, for example, Kafka is exploring the themes of being different, being alone and confused. The writer's ideas emerge from the characters and how they behave, the events and thoughts in a story, and from the story-teller's comments.

Activity Write a story of your own where you feel left out or different from the people round about you. Try to put across the themes of loneliness and confusion.

Follow-up
- For help on planning and drafting, see pages 62–63.
- For help on imaginative writing, see pages 76–77.

Setting and Atmosphere

Setting the Scene

Setting the scene in a story or play is always an important part of how ideas and characters are going to develop. The surroundings are usually carefully chosen by the author and they are often the starting point for creating a particular mood or atmosphere.

Here is the start of Chapter 3 of *Great Expectations* by Charles Dickens. It is told from the point of view of a young boy called Pip.

Great Expectations

It was a rimy morning and very damp. I had seen the damp lying on the outside of my little window, as if some goblin had been crying there all night, and using the window for a pocket handkerchief. Now, I saw the damp lying on the bare hedges and spare grass, like a coarser sort of spiders' webs; hanging itself from twig to twig and blade to blade. On every rail and gate, wet lay clammy; and the marsh-mist was so thick, that the wooden finger on the post directing people to our village – a direction which they never accepted, for they never came there – was invisible to me until I was quite close under it. Then, as I looked up at it, while it dripped, it seemed to my oppressed conscience like a phantom devoting me to the Hulks.

The mist was heavier yet when I got out upon the marshes, so that instead of my running at everything, everything seemed to run at me. This was very disagreeable to a guilty mind. The gates and dykes and banks came bursting at me through the mist, as if they cried as plainly as could be, 'A boy with Somebody-else's pork pie! Stop him!' The cattle came upon me with like suddenness, staring out of their eyes, and steaming out of their nostrils, 'Holloa, young thief!' One black ox, with a white cravat on – who even had to my awakened conscience something of a clerical air – fixed me so obstinately with his eyes, and moved his blunt head round in such an accusatory manner as I moved round, that I blubbered out to him, 'I couldn't help it, sir!' It wasn't for myself I took it!' Upon which, he put down his head, blew a cloud of smoke out of his nose, and vanished with a kick-up of his hind legs and a flourish of his tail.

Charles Dickens

Activity

1 The setting, atmosphere, and Pip's mood are very closely linked. See what details you can find by drawing your own version of the chart below and filling it in.

	Evidence from the passage
Setting	
Time of day	
Mood and atmosphere	
Pip's state of mind	

2 Draw a sequence of pictures that capture the extract's mood and atmosphere and try to find ways of showing what Pip might be thinking or feeling.

3 Write a report of what you have attempted to show and why. What links can you find between the atmosphere and Pip's state of mind?

Working on

1 Pip has been threatened and forced to steal. Write your own scene, keeping a similar atmosphere to that in *Great Expectations*, but choose a completely different setting, e.g. in a town, a shop, a school, a club, etc. Write it from the point of view of the person who is committing the theft.

2 Use the same basic characters and setting, but now write the scene from the point of view of the victim of the theft. The mood and atmosphere will change.

Follow-up

• For more help on imaginative writing, see pages 76–77.

Characters

Understanding Characters

When we meet people in real life, we often form an impression of what they are like depending on how they look and how they behave – from their clothes, their hair, their face, how they talk, how they walk, and other mannerisms.

In plays, stories, and poems too we judge the characters we are introduced to, but here we rely on how an author describes them and feels about them, how they are made to move, speak, and behave.

Below is a passage from *Carrie's War* where Carrie and Nick meet Miss Evans and hear about her brother.

Carrie's War

'Call me Auntie,' Miss Evans said. 'Auntie Louise. Or Auntie Lou, if that's easier. But you'd best call my brother Mr Evans. You see, he's a Councillor.' She paused and then went on in the same proud tone she had used when she showed them the bathroom, 'Mr Evans is a very important man. He's at a Council meeting just now. I think I'd best give you supper before he comes back, hadn't I?'

They had a good supper of eggs and milk and crunchy, fresh bread in the kitchen which was as clean as the rest of the house but more cheerful with a big range fire that threw out heat like a furnace. Miss Evans didn't eat with them but stood by the table like a waitress in a restaurant, taking the plates to the sink as soon as they'd cleared them and sweeping up crumbs round their chairs before they had finished drinking their milk. She didn't actually say, 'Please hurry up, oh please hurry up,' but she might just as well have done: her mouth twitched as if she were muttering it inwardly, her eyes kept darting to the clock on the mantelpiece and there were red, nervous spots on her cheeks.

She made the children nervous too. When she said, 'What about bed, now?' they were more than glad to escape from the kitchen where the Very Important Councillor Evans might appear any minute. As they went upstairs, Miss Evans rolled up the drugget behind them. 'Mr Evans doesn't like to see it down,' she explained when she caught Carrie's eye. 'I just put it there while he's out to keep the carpet spick and span. It's a new one, you see, lovely deep pile, and Mr Evans doesn't want it trodden on.'

'How are you supposed to get up the stairs, then?' Nick said. 'Walk on the ceiling, or fly like a bird?'

… Miss Evans laughed, rather breathlessly. 'Of course you have to walk on it sometimes but not too often. Mr Evans said twice a day would be quite enough. You see, four of us going up and down twice a day, morning and evening, makes 16 times altogether, and Mr Evans thinks that's quite enough traipsing so if you could try to remember to bring down all the things you'll want for the day, in the morning …'

'But the *bathroom's* upstairs,' Nick said in an outraged voice.

She looked at him apologetically. 'Yes, I know, dear. But if you want to – you know – *go anywhere*, there's one at the end of the yard. Mr Evans doesn't use it, of course, it wouldn't be dignified for him to be seen going there, not a man in his position, when all the neighbours know he's got one indoors, but *I* use it, and though it's an earth closet it's quite nice and clean.'

Nina Bawden

Activity

We build up our understanding of a character in a number of ways, by actions, words, and looks. What have you found out about Miss Evans so far? Write a Personal Profile for her by drawing your own version of the chart below. List all the details you can find and include short quotations from the passage to support what you are saying.

Name	
Voice	
Appearance	
Behaviour	
Setting	
Other features	
Your opinion of the character	

Working on

Construct the character of Mr Evans from what you have learned from the extract. Build up a Personal Profile sheet on him before you begin, adding your own details so you have a clear picture in your imagination of the sort of person he is.

Compare your version of his character with the one that emerges in the extract from *Carrie's War* on pages 108–109.

Follow-up

- For help reading for detail, see pages 44–45.
- For help on quoting from a text, see pages 114–115.

Narrative Technique

Objectives:

- to learn about different methods an author can use in telling a story
- to develop an understanding of writing in the first and third person

Putting a Story Together

Narrative technique involves the methods a writer uses to put a story together. (These have been explored in previous units.) It is concerned with:

- how the story, plot, and themes are developed
- how the setting and atmosphere are created
- how the characters are constructed
- the sort of language an author chooses
- who tells the story in the book – the authorial voice

Authorial Voice

The author of a story makes a deliberate choice about how that story will be told and who will tell it, and this has a great impact on the nature of the narrative. The story can be told:

- in the **first person**, through the eyes of a main character in the story (like Pip in *Great Expectations*)
- in the **third person**, as if somebody has reported events that have happened (as in a newspaper report)
- from the point of view of an **omniscient narrator**, where the person telling the story knows everything that is going on inside all the characters' heads (as in *Carrie's War*)

Writing in the first person

If a story is written in the first person, it is written from the particular point of view of the character telling the story. Although it gives events a ring of truth, a reader has no first-hand knowledge of what others in the story are thinking. The passage below is written in the first person from Rebecca's point of view.

Your Friend Rebecca

She calls him 'he' – not 'Dad'.

Later on I have my tea and leave his in the oven on a plate. It'll get dry and shrivelled up, but he won't say anything.

What does she feel here?

It serves him right. I usually make the tea early because sometimes he comes straight home from work and we sit down together, staring at each other. Not knowing what to say. But most days, like now, he's late and I have my tea

What does this suggest?

first. When he comes in then I'm watching the television or pretending to do some homework upstairs, and then we don't have to talk to each other at all. I think I like it best that way.

Linda Hoy

Activity How does Rebecca feel about her father? How do you know this? –
what does she call him? What does she say about him? What does she
do? Try writing about these incidents from her father's point of view.

Writing in the third person

Writing in the third person is more like writing a report – as an
outsider looking on. A reader has no idea what any of the characters
are thinking – it is all guesswork. The following extract starts in the
third person with a description of a boy, Ralph, on a beach.

Lord of the Flies

The boy with the fair hair lowered himself down the last few
feet of rock and began to pick his way towards the lagoon.
Though he had taken off his school sweater and trailed it
now from one hand, his grey shirt stuck to him and his hair
plastered to his forehead. All round him the long scar
smashed into the jungle was a bath of heat. He was
clambering heavily among the creepers and broken trunks
when a bird, a vision of red and yellow, flashed upwards
with a witch-like cry …

Writing as an omniscient narrator

As the story continues, the narrative technique begins to change and
the reader is drawn into the story by sharing Ralph's thoughts and
feelings. This is the technique of omniscient narration.

Beyond the platform there was more enchantment. Some
act of God – a typhoon perhaps, or the storm that had
accompanied his own arrival – had banked sand inside the
lagoon so that there was a long, deep pool in the beach with
a high ledge of pink granite at the further end. Ralph had
been deceived before now by the specious appearance of
depth in a beach pool and he approached this one preparing
to be disappointed. But the island ran true to form and the
incredible pool, which clearly was only invaded by the sea at
high tide, was so deep at one end as to be dark green. Ralph
inspected the whole 30 yards carefully and then plunged in.
The water was warmer than his blood and he might have
been swimming in a huge bath.

William Golding

*We begin to share
his feelings.*

Activity 1 Rewrite the opening passages from *Lord of the Flies* in the first
person, as if you were Ralph.
2 Write the extract from *Your Friend Rebecca* from the point of view
of an omniscient narrator.

Which writing technique do you prefer? Why?

Follow-up • For more help on writing in the first or third person, see page 70.

Style in Prose

Keeping Your Interest

An author will use a number of devices to keep the reader interested in a story or character, such as irony, flashback, and suspense.

Irony

When used in speech, irony is saying the opposite of what you really mean.

Well, you have been a good boy, haven't you!

In writing, irony is often used to make the reader think more carefully about the motives and morals of characters in a story. It can work like a form of shared secret between the reader and either a character or the narrator, whereby they can understand something better than some of those actually involved in what is going on.

In the extract below, a careful reader will see through Napoleon's behaviour in a way that the other characters cannot.

Animal Farm

The milk seems unimportant to him – he's up to something.

He encourages them to go to work, but he stays behind on his own.

Nobody says anything but it would seem that Napoleon has taken all the milk for himself.

'What is going to happen to all that milk?' said someone.
'Jones used sometimes to mix some of it in our mash,' said one of the hens.
'Never mind the milk, comrades,' cried Napoleon, placing himself in front of the buckets. 'That will be attended to. The harvest is more important. Comrade Snowball will lead the way. I shall follow in a few minutes. Forward, comrades! The hay is waiting.'
So the animals trooped down to the hayfield to begin the harvest, and when they came back in the evening it was noticed that the milk had disappeared.

George Orwell

Flashback

All stories rely on time, often following a sequence of events from a to b to c, etc. Sometimes, to keep the reader interested or to create a sort of narrative puzzle to challenge the reader, an author will alter the normal sequence of events. This can be done in two ways:
- looking back at an earlier event
- slipping into a different period of time

In the following extract from *The Midnight Fox* by Betsy Byars, Tommy looks back at an earlier event:

> Sometimes at night when the rain is beating against the windows of my room, I think about that summer on the farm ... Or sometimes it is that last terrible night, and I am standing beneath

the oak tree with the rain beating against me ... Then it seems to me that I can hear, as plainly as I heard it that August night, above the rain, beyond the years, the high, clear bark of the midnight fox.

In the following extract from *Tom's Midnight Garden* by Philippa Pearce, Tom discovers he can slip back in time:

One night when the clock struck thirteen, Tom found that although he was still in the same house, he had slipped back in time, into the distant past.

Suspense

Suspense is another way of keeping interest. It is created whenever a reader wants to find out what will happen next in a story. A writer will usually build up suspense by appealing to the senses – particularly of sight, sound, touch, and feeling. Look at the following passage when Tom finds himself in another world:

Tom's Midnight Garden

He came out upon the lawn again. Here were the flower-beds – the crescent-shaped corner-beds with the hyacinths, among which an early bee was already working ...

At the verge of the lawn, Tom stopped abruptly. On the grey-green of the dewed grass were two clearly defined patches of darker green: footprints. Feet had walked on that lawn and stood there; then they had turned back and walked off again. How long ago? Surely since Tom had entered the garden. 'I'm sure they weren't here when I came out. Certain.'

How long had whoever it was stood there, and why? He or she had faced the line of yew-trees opposite; and that thought made Tom uneasy. When he had passed behind those trees and seen the flick-flick-flick of the house between them, had someone stood on the lawn watching the flick-flick-flick of Tom as he went?

Tom looked at the house, letting his eye go from window to window. Had someone drawn out of sight at an upper window? No, no: now he was just imagining things.

Tom's nerves were on edge, and he actually jumped when he heard a noise from up the garden. It was the sound of a door opening ...

Philippa Pearce

Activity

1 Taking notes from the passage, draw up a chart of:
   what happens: sights, sounds, and feelings. Also make notes on how the choice of language affects the changing pace of the extract.
2 Write your own short story where you try to use suspense – perhaps it might end on a cliff-hanger.

Follow-up

- For help on reading for detail, see pages 44–45
- For more on imaginative writing, see pages 76–77.
- For more on setting and atmosphere, see pages 88–89.

Reading Prose

Working on a Story

The passage below is from *Buddy* by Nigel Hinton. Buddy and his two friends have heard that a local house is haunted. A murder took place there some years previously, and a strange man they have nick-named the Beast seems to live in the house. They decide to investigate.

Buddy

The three steps that led down to the back door were shiny with damp. To the right of the door was a window that, like those at the front, had been boarded-up. Just to the left of the door, though, about seven feet from the ground was a small window that not only had no boards on it but was actually half-open. He (Buddy) caught hold of the window-sill …

Buddy swung the window outwards and hauled himself up until his head and shoulders were through the hole. He was now blocking most of the light but he could see that the small room had been some kind of larder …

He kicked his legs and started to squirm through. It was a tight squeeze and he grazed his shin, but finally he managed to pull his body through. Balancing with one hand on the shelf and the other on the window ledge, he jumped to the floor. His leg stung like mad. He lifted his jeans and wiped a trickle of blood from the graze.

He was just reaching for the doorknob when it started to turn. Someone was in the house. He sprang round and leaped for the window. His hands slipped and he tumbled backwards on to the floor.

Julius was grinning down at him. 'The back door wasn't locked.'

Buddy took a few seconds to get his breath back then let Julius pull him to his feet. He followed him out into the corridor where Charmian was slowly opening another door opposite. The room was in semi-darkness because of the boards on the window. Buddy tried the switch just inside the door but no light came on. In the corner near the window he could just make out an old-fashioned, shallow, stone sink into which a tap dripped softly. Along the far wall an ancient gas stove lay on its side as if someone had disconnected it and then let it drop.

'This must be where he sleeps,' Charmian said in a rather scared voice.

Buddy turned and looked at the camp bed that stood against the wall behind the door. There were a couple of blankets on it and a rolled-up sweater that obviously served as a pillow. All along the bed stood candles of various sizes. Was the Beast scared of the dark? …

The front room on the right of the hall was a mess. The wallpaper was hanging off the walls and there were chunks of fallen plaster on the floor. The room on the left of the hall, though, looked as if someone had swept it recently. It was completely empty except that in the middle of

the bare floorboards there was a telephone.

'Why put it there?' Charmian asked.

'Why have one at all?' Julius answered. 'The whole place is weird. I wonder where he killed her?'...

Julius led the way up the staircase to the first floor ... There was a chink of glass and Buddy glanced up and saw Julius stumble. A bottle shot out from under his foot and came tumbling down towards them. Buddy tried to stop it but it caught the edge of the stair above him and flipped over his hand. It sailed on a high arc and shattered on the tiles of the hall. The crash could have been heard out in the street.

In the silence afterwards, they all held their breath.

'Blimey, this is scaring,' Julius said at last. 'Let's have a quick look up here then get out.' ...

There were high windows at either end of the attic ... As he (Buddy) wiped the dust from the window a huge spider scuttled over the glass. He sprang back ... A sudden scurry of wind brought the rain beating down so heavily that the houses across the street became just dim shapes. Something moved in the garden ... The Beast was walking fast across the lawn.

Nigel Hinton

Activity

1 Make a chart like the one below and for each section record quotations from the extract. Occasionally you might need to read between the lines, e.g. we are never told directly that Buddy is very frightened, but there are many descriptive details that suggest he is. Note: For the 'Style' category, look at how the suspense is developed.

Characters	
Their feelings and emotions	
Setting	
Mood and atmosphere	
Style	
What makes the passage effective?	

2 Using the ideas you have gathered, write a critical report about the passage as a whole. Make sure you use a separate paragraph for each area or topic you write about.

Follow-up
- For help on characters, see pages 90–91.
- For help on setting and atmosphere, see pages 88–89.
- For help on aspects of style in prose, see pages 94–95.

Style in Poetry

Objectives:

- to help you understand some of the 'tools' a poet can use
- to give you an opportunity to develop some of these skills

Poetry Techniques

In writing a poem a poet may use a variety of techniques to produce certain effects and create meanings. For example:

- words may be carefully chosen (*diction*)
- certain technical devices might be used (*imagery* – simile, metaphor)
- the words on the page might be arranged or punctuated in special ways (*sentence variety*)
- the poet may have a noticeable point of view (*tone*)

but it is the overall meaning of the poem that the reader must get to grips with. Always try and understand a poem as a whole – see what it is about and then work through it to see how that meaning has been put across. This approach should be reflected in any writing you do about the poem.

Frogs

Frogs sit more solid
Than anything sits. In mid-leap they are
Parachutists falling
In a free fall. They die on roads
With arms across their chests and
Heads high.

I love frogs that sit
Like Buddha, that fall without
Parachutes, that die
Like Italian tenors.

Above all, I love them because,
Pursued in water, they never
Panic so much that they fail
To make stylish triangles
With their ballet dancer's
Legs.
            Norman MacCaig

Activity

1 Read the poem *Frogs* carefully. What are your first impressions? What did you enjoy about it most? Can you give one word to describe the poem?

2 Now try to write a report on the poem. Bear in mind the following points:

Content

- What is the poem about?
- What people or things are involved?
- What is being described?

Tone

- When reading the poem through, can you hear the poet's mood?
- What do you think his point of view is about frogs and how can you tell this?

Sentence variety

- How has the poem been set out on the page? Why do you think this is?
- Are any particular words or ideas emphasized by the way the lines have been arranged?
- Why do you think that none of the lines are end-stopped, so that the lines and meanings run-on (spill over to the next line)?
- Is there anything interesting about the punctuation?

Diction

- What sort of words has the poet chosen? Why do you think this is?
- Are there any rhymes – at the end of lines or internal rhymes within lines?
- Which words have been repeated? Why do you think this is?
- Can you find where the poet has used alliteration (repeating the same consonant) or assonance (repeating vowel sounds)? What ideas or words does this draw attention to?
- Is there any onomatopoeia (where the sound of something is linked to its name)?

Imagery

Metaphors and similes – images which create word pictures by using comparisons – can both be found in this poem.
- What similes (where one thing is compared to another using the words *as* or *like*) can you find?
- What metaphors (where one thing is described directly *as* something else) can you find?

Working on

Try writing a poem on a subject of your own choice or on one of the following: school, a best friend, going to the dentist, an embarrassing moment.

Follow-up

- For a fuller explanation of technical words and terms, see Glossary on pages 126–127.
- For more on reading poetry, see the following unit.

Reading Poetry

More Than Meets the Eye

Poetry often uses a compressed form of language and explores powerful and intense human experiences. The poem below has more to it than meets the eye at first. Start by reading it, at least twice, slowly and carefully.

Mort Aux Chats

There will be no more cats.
Cats spread infection,
cats pollute the air,
cats consume seven times
their own weight in food a week,
cats were worshipped in
decadent societies (Egypt
and Ancient Rome), The Greeks
had no use for cats. Cats
sit down to pee (our scientists
have proved it). The copulation
of cats is harrowing; they
are unbearably fond of the moon.

Perhaps they are all right in
their own country but their
traditions are alien to ours.
Cats smell, they can't help it,
you notice it going upstairs.
Cats watch too much television,
they can sleep through storms,
they stabbed us in the back
last time. There have never been
any great artists who were cats.
They don't deserve a capital C
except at the beginning of a sentence.
I blame my headache and my
plants dying on to cats.
Our district is full of them,
property values are falling.
When I dream of God I see
a Massacre of Cats. Why
should they insist on their own
language and religion, who
needs to purr to make his point?
Death to all cats! The Rule
of Dogs shall last a thousand years!

Peter Porter

> This poem is <u>cruel</u>!

> The person who wrote this must have hated cats!

> I think it's funny and fun to read.

> He tries to give cats a bad name.

> The poet sounds very aggressive and angry.

> I don't think it's about cats at all!

Activity

1 What are your first impressions of the poem (surface meanings)?
Write down your ideas as you read the poem through.
   • What does the poem seem to be about?
   • Which are fair criticisms? What is true?
   • Which are unfair criticism? What is false?
   • Is there anything you find funny in this poem?

2 What do you notice about the way it has been written –
the poem's style? Write your ideas and comments down.
   • How has the poem been set out?
   • What sort of words has the poet chosen?
   • What do you notice about the way it has been punctuated?
   • Does it read like a poem? If not, why not?
   • What words or phrases stand out? Why?
   • Is there anything that surprises you?

Working on

1 What are your second impressions (deeper meanings)?
   • Is this poem just about cats? What else could it be about?
   • What happens to the ideas if you leave a gap every time the word
     'cats' appears?
   • Can you substitute other words, filling the gaps with a particular
     type or group of people?

2 Imagine the author of this poem reading it aloud.
   • Is he trying to make his audience laugh?
   • Is he trying to puzzle us?
   • Is he trying to make us think?
   • What tone of voice would he use?

3 What are your final impressions? You may be coming to the
conclusion that the poet is stating something quite different from
what he really means – that he is using irony.
   • What do you think the subject of the poem is now?
   • What do you think Peter Porter's attitude is to the subject of
     his poem?
   • Why do you think Peter Porter chose to make his protest against
     racism in the form of a poem like this?

4 Write a letter to the author expressing your views about the poem.
Try to include the ideas you have been working on in the sections
above.

Follow-up
   • For help on the use of irony, see page 94.
   • For more help on aspects of style in poetry, see pages 98–99.
   • For other poems dealing with prejudice, see the following: *Say This City Has Ten Million
     Souls* by W H Auden; *Dumb Insolence* by Adrian Mitchell; *The Telephone Conversation*
     by Wole Soyinka; *I Sit and Look Out* by Walt Whitman; *As Others See Us* by Basil
     Dowling; *She Said* by Liz Hutchins; *Tish Miller* by Wendy Cope; *Foreign* by Carol Ann Duffy

Reading Shakespeare

Shakespeare's Language

Shakespeare wrote his plays about 400 years ago. He produced some of the most popular plays of his day and attracted thousands to the theatre to see them performed.

Inevitably some words in his scripts have changed their meanings or spellings in the last four centuries. The order of words in a sentence may also be different from the order we use today.

However, whether you are watching one of Shakespeare's plays or reading one, the basic approach to understanding the language is the same – do not worry about understanding every single word, but try to get a general impression or idea of what is going on and how the characters are feeling and reacting.

Reading *Hamlet*

Look at the following extract from the opening scene of Shakespeare's *Hamlet*. When the play opens, King Hamlet of Denmark has recently died. Some soldiers are on night-watch on the castle battlements and they are nervous because for the past two nights they have seen a ghost. They have persuaded Horatio to join them to see the ghost for himself and when it appears again, they realize that it is the ghost of the dead king.

Hamlet

Bernardo: Welcome, Horatio; Welcome, good Marcellus.
Horatio: What, has this thing appear'd again tonight? —— In a teasing manner?
Bernardo: I have seen nothing.
Marcellus: Horatio says 'tis but our fantasy,
And will not let belief take hold of him } Much more serious.
Touching this dreaded sight, twice seen of us;
Therefore I have entreated him along
With us to watch the minutes of this night,
That, if again this apparition come,
He may approve our eyes[1] and speak to it.
Horatio: Tush, tush, 'twill not appear.
Bernardo: Sit down awhile, ———————————— Where should they sit?
And let us once again assail your ears,
That are so fortified against our story,
What we have two nights seen.
Horatio: Well, sit we down,
And let us hear Bernardo speak of this. — Does this suggest a starry night?
Bernardo: Last night of all,
When yond same star that's westward from the pole
Had made his course t'illume that part of heaven

Where now it burns, Marcellus and myself, — He stops abruptly.
The bell then beating one – ———

How should the ghost be walking?

(*Enter Ghost.*)

Marcellus: Peace, break thee off; look where it comes again. ⎫
Bernardo: In the same figure, like the King that's dead.   ⎬ How should they
Marcellus: Thou art a scholar; speak to it, Horatio.   show their fear
Bernardo: Looks 'a[2] not like the King? Mark it, Horatio. ⎭ and the sudden
                                                                change of mood?
 Horatio: Most like. It harrows me with fear and wonder.
Bernardo: It would be spoke to.
Marcellus: Question it, Horatio. ———————————— Should he start to
                                                    move forward?
 Horatio: What art <u>thou</u>[3] that usurp'st this time of night
            Together with that fair and warlike form ——— Should the ghost
            In which the majesty of buried Denmark   be wearing
            Did sometimes march?   armour?
            By heaven I charge <u>thee</u>[4], speak!
Marcellus: It is offended. ————————————————— Why?
Bernardo: See, it stalks away.
 Horatio: Stay! Speak, speak! I charge thee, speak! ——— Does he follow the
                                                            ghost?

(*Exit Ghost.*)

William Shakespeare

Footnotes
[1] confirm what we have seen   [2] he
[3] pronoun meaning 'you'   [4] pronoun meaning 'you'

Activity Make a detailed study of the scene as if you were planning to stage it,
making the sort of comments, sketches, and diagrams that a producer
would make to help the actors interpret the scene on stage. The
questions and comments marked around the script above might help.
You need to decide:
- how and when the characters are going to move
- what sort of lighting will be appropriate
- the sort of costumes the characters will wear
- how the lines should be spoken and which words need to be stressed
- how the characters should interact with each other

Follow-up • For more on playscripts, see the following unit.

Modern Playscripts

The Shape of Plays

Stories and plays help us to picture life in a variety of ways – as it is, as it could be, or as we might like it to be.

Most plays open with a specific setting or background where characters are presented in a normal, undisrupted situation. Quite soon after the beginning some sort of problem or event arises which upsets the way things have been. The bulk of the play explores or develops this problem, until some sort of solution is arrived at in the end. In exploring the problem, the author often brings certain ideas and themes about life to our attention.

In the play *The Granny Project* by Anne Fine, the characters Sophie, Nicholas, Tanya, and Ivan are determined that they will not allow their parents (Natasha and Henry) to go ahead with plans to put their grandmother in a home. They decide to make their school Social Science project focus on ageing people in the community to make their parents feel ashamed of what they are planning to do. They are delighted when they succeed and their parents agree that Granny can stay – as long as all copies of the project are destroyed. However, the scheme goes wrong and Ivan ends up having to look after his grandmother by himself.

The play takes place in a large, untidy family kitchen and living area. On one side, in front of the oven, sink and fridge, stands a table surrounded by stools. On the other, two tatty armchairs and a few floor cushions are grouped around a television.

The Granny Project

Natasha: Ivan has made his own position entirely clear. His Granny must be cared for in this house. Right?

Ivan: (*Suspicious*) Right.

Natasha: Fine. Very well. It is agreed. The Granny Project has been burned. Granny stays here. And Ivan himself will do all the caring.

Sophie: What?

Tanya: Ivan?

Nicholas: By himself?

Ivan: Me?

Natasha: You.

Ivan: What do you mean, exactly – do all the caring?

Natasha: (*Airily*) Oh, you know. You've seen your father and me do it for nine years. Taking trays in and out ten times a day. Fetching and carrying. Bed changing. Laundering. Medicine giving. Sewing on buttons. Fetching her pension. Buying her peppermints. Changing her television channel. Filling her hot water bottles. Sitting with her for hours. Keeping her room warm. Switching on her lamps when it gets dark and switching them off again when she falls asleep. Tuning her radio. Finding her spectacles. Picking up her book. Closing her window. Opening her window. Drawing her curtains. Writing her few remaining Christmas cards. Consoling her when her friends die. Reminding her to eat … Why are you staring at me? Have I missed something?

Ivan: I have to do all that? By myself?

Natasha: Do as you please. Share it between the four of you or do it yourself. You care so much. You can arrange it.

Sophie: What about you and dad?

Natasha: We will take over your jobs, of course.

Nicholas: Our jobs? What jobs?

Natasha: Oh, you know. Popping in to see her whenever the other television is blinking. Worrying about her going into a Home. Putting heads round the door to say goodnight, when you remember. I think it sums it up. Have I missed something?

Tanya: You're **joking**. You must be.

Natasha: (*Striking her hand on the table*) **Not joking. I am not joking.**

Sophie: But …

Natasha: No buts! No buts, no backsliding. The first time I hear a grumble, she goes!
(*Silence. Then Ivan laughs.*)

Ivan: Blackmail! Checkmate! You win! Congratulations!
(*Natasha smiles modestly and extends her hand. He leans over and kisses it.*)

Anne Fine

Activity

1 Examine the way this scene has been written. Make notes about how the following have been used and how they are effective:
- different length speeches
- stage directions
- the flow of conversation

2 Make detailed notes on the following points and then, using the information you have gathered, write a diary entry for Ivan about the crisis that he might have made. Try to include as much relevant information as you can.
- What picture of family life does the play give us? (You will need to look at what the characters are like and the setting.)
- What is the problem they have to work through?
- What is the solution that appears to have been reached? Do you think it will work?
- What ideas about family life could the author be exploring?

Follow-up
- For more help on script layout, see page 40.
- For help on reading for detail, see pages 44–45.
- For help on making notes, see page 48.
- For help on writing diary entries, see pages 50–51.

Assignment: Comparing Genres 1

Warning

When I am an old woman I shall wear purple
With a red hat which doesn't go, and doesn't suit me,
And I shall spend my pension on brandy and summer gloves
And satin sandals, and say we've no money for butter.
I shall sit down on the pavement when I'm tired
And gobble up samples in shops and press alarm bells
And run my stick along the public railings
And make up for the sobriety of my youth.
I shall go out in my slippers in the rain
And pick the flowers from other people's gardens,
And learn to spit.

You can wear terrible shirts and grow more fat
And eat three pounds of sausages at a go
Or only bread and pickle for a week
And hoard pens and pencils and beermats and things in boxes.

But now we must have clothes that keep us dry
And pay our rent and not swear in the street,
And set a good example for the children.
We will have friends to dinner and read the papers.

But maybe I ought to practise a little now?
So people are not too shocked and surprised
When suddenly I am old and start to wear purple.

Jenny Joseph

Gran

I liked Gran; she was so different from mum ... While she talked to me, she washed her face and hands in a large mixing bowl which she stood on the kitchen table and was filled to the brim with boiling water. The red, strong-smelling soap rested on a saucer while she covered her face with a creamy pink lather, then sluiced it off, cupping her hands several times with water and sounding, as she put her face into it, as though she were drinking a bowl of soup. With water dripping from her chins and her eyes stinging with soap, she groped around blindly for the towel, tugging first at the tablecloth, then at the curtains, until she realized that it was still hanging on the line over the range ...

Finally, she combed her grey, greasy hair that was usually lank, but if she was going to a special jumble sale that day, or to her old age pensioners' club, she forced it to curl by using her iron curling tongs. She would sit in her armchair and wait for the tortuous tongs to turn red-hot in the fire then, catching a strand of hair in a scorching grasp, she twisted the tongs round and round until they could go no further ...

(from *London Morning* by Valerie Avery)

The Granny Project

Sophie: You learned a lot from Granny, didn't you?...

Ivan: Well... She talked quite a bit about being old ... She said that for the first time in her life, she had time to herself. Time to sit quietly and watch the plants grow, she said. Time to keep still so all the birds came near. She said some days she sat in her chair and watched Natasha rushing about pegging sheets on the washing line, and then she would sit quietly the livelong day, and watch them dry.

Sophie: Watched them dry? All day?

Ivan: And listened ...

Sophie: Listened?

Ivan: That's what she said. She listened to them flapping in the wind. (*He waves his hands in the air*) Flap-flap, flap-flap. That's what she said. She said if you get to sit quietly in a house for long enough, you get to feel a part of it.

Sophie: I'll never be like that.

Ivan: That's what she said. She thought she'd never be like that. She said all those years when she and grandfather would stay up till all hours doing the union work, fighting the battles over pay, and conditions, and health insurance, she never thought of simply living her life with him quietly, alone, just being together like two companionable cows in a field.

Sophie: If there's work to be done, you have to do it, simply because it's there, still waiting to be done.

Ivan: Oh, yes. But she says they weren't hard-boiled revolutionaries. They were soft souls.

Sophie: Soft souls?

Ivan: She meant that they were proud of little things. Like the fact children don't cough all through the winters any more, or walk around crying from chilblains. She said making things better is sad, slow work, and you have to be very careful not to mix it up with fancy ideas.

Sophie: Fancy ideas?

Ivan: Like being a revolutionary, or something.

Sophie: You always have to keep the chilblains in mind?

Ivan: I think that's what she meant. Always to remember what's going to mean the most to most people.

Anne Fine

Activity Compare the different views we are given of old age in the above passages. Which of the passages has left you with the strongest sense of what being old is like? Why is this?

Before writing your comparison, gather some words and phrases from each extract – ideally direct quotations – for the following categories:

- appearance of main character
- personal qualities
- relationships with others
- how they feel about their life
- any special language used
- themes

You can then use these details when you write your comparison.

Follow-up
- For help on reading for detail, see pages 44–45.
- For help on quoting from a text, see pages 114–115.

Character Analysis

Reading Carefully

The starting point for any close work with a text must be careful reading. The earlier unit on 'Characters' (pages 90-91) showed you how to understand a character by looking at Miss Evans from *Carrie's War* by Nina Bawden. Carrie and Nick had been evacuated to the Evans's house. The story continues with details about Miss Evans's brother, and how the children feel about him at first.

Carrie's War

Miss Evans was standing outside. 'Into bed now,' she said softly, hustling them past her. Then she began scuttering backwards and forwards like a small, frightened mouse, picking up the things they had dropped, clothes in the bedroom, toothpaste tube in the bathroom. 'Oh dear,' she was saying, under her breath, 'oh dear, oh dear, oh dear …'

'Lou,' a man's voice shouted. 'Lou! What are you up to?'

'Coming, Samuel,' Miss Evans called from the landing. 'Just a minute.'

'What are you doing up there? I might have known, I suppose. Up and down the stairs, soon as my back's turned, wearing out the stair carpet …'

Safe in bed, Carrie blew out the candle. Miss Evans shut the door.

… The loud, hectoring voice went on. 'Messing and humbugging about, up and down, back and forth, in and out, messing and humbugging about …'

It was velvet dark in the room, no light from the window because the thick, blackout curtains were drawn. They lay quite still in the darkness, listening to the roar of Mr Evans's voice and the thin squeak of his sister's. Like a mouse answering a lion, Carrie thought. Then the heavy tread of feet down the passage. The bang of another door. And silence at last …

… (Nick) was shaking and shivering. He whispered into her ear, 'He must be an Ogre, Carrie. A horrible, disgusting, real-life OGRE.'

He wasn't an Ogre, of course. Just a tall, thin, cross man with a loud voice, pale, staring, pop-eyes, and tufts of spiky hair sticking out from each nostril.

Councillor Samuel Isaac Evans was a bully. He bullied his sister. He even bullied the women who came into his shop, selling them things they didn't really want to buy and refusing to stock things that they did. 'Take it or leave it,' he'd say. 'Don't you know there's a war on?'

He would have bullied the children if he had thought they were frightened of him. But although Carrie was a little frightened, she didn't show it, and Nick wasn't frightened at all. He was frightened of Ogres and spiders and crabs and cold water and the dentist and dark nights, but he wasn't frightened of people. Perhaps this was only because he had never had reason to be until he met Mr Evans, but he wasn't afraid of him, even after that first, dreadful night, because Mr Evans had false teeth that clicked when he talked. 'You can't really be scared of someone whose teeth might fall out,' he told Carrie.

Nina Bawden

Activity

1 Read the above passage again and this time make notes on all the details you can find out about Mr Evans that answer the following questions. Include short quotations from the passage to support what you are saying.

What facts are you told?
- What do you know about the character's name and background?
- List the details of his appearance and habits.
- Describe his personality.
- What does he seem to think of other people and himself?
- How does he behave?

How are you told these things?
- What is told from the author's point of view?
- What do you learn through opinions and comments from the characters?
- What do you learn through what happens – actions as well as conversations and thoughts?

2 Now compare your findings with the work you did on the character of Mr Evans on pages 90–91. What has changed?

Working on

You should look for several additional points in the two passages on *Carrie's War* (pages 90–91 and 108–109):
- Which characters change and develop? In what ways? Why?
- Which characters stay the same?
- Are the characters believable? If not, why not?
- If yes, how has the author made them realistic?
- Are any of the characters similar to yourself in any way?

1 Write the diary entry that Mr Evans might have made when Carrie and Nick first arrived in his house. Try to get inside his personality.
2 Write a detailed character study of Mr Evans, using the information collected in the Activity above. Remember to organize your work into paragraphs.

Follow-up
- For information about the characters in *Carrie's War*, see pages 90–91.
- For help on quoting from a text, see pages 114–115.
- For help on writing diary entries, see pages 50–51.

Major Themes

Facts and Ideas

When anyone asks what a story is about, there is more than one way of replying. You could:

- give the key incidents that are vital to the story
- outline the main themes – the ideas in the story
- do both

Read the following excerpts from the blurb about the book *Sumitra's Story* by Rukshana Smith. Both the facts and the themes of the story are presented.

Facts of the story

'When Sumitra's family are thrown out of Uganda by President Amin they go to live in England. At school and work Sumitra mixes with people of different backgrounds and nationalities and she finds it increasingly difficult to accept her parents' strict Hindu values. Sumitra has a difficult choice to make.'

Exploration of themes

'Sumitra is encouraged to be free-thinking and independent. She *rebels* against the idea of an arranged marriage and a pre-ordained life-style. Finding herself increasingly torn between strict values and liberal attitudes, she struggles to establish her own identity, her own future.'

These two paragraphs come from the publisher's information about the book, but did not appear under two separate headings. From the key words and phrases highlighted, a reader can see that the book is likely to explore a variety of ideas:

- culture clashes
- the generation gap
- growing up
- rebellion
- the search for identity
- intolerance
- freedom
- prejudice
- feeling different
- making choices

Activity

1 Think of a story you know well – perhaps one from your childhood. (*Sleeping Beauty* or *Aladdin* might be possibilities.) Try to tell the whole story in just six short numbered sentences, leaving out less important events that simply add interest and more detail. These should be the key incidents of the story.

2 Draw these key incidents in cartoon form with captions underneath explaining what is happening.

3 Look at your cartoon drawings again and see which themes you think might be important at each key incident. Certain themes crop up again and again in stories, such as:

love   fear   loneliness   greed   friendship
poverty   freedom   money   good   evil

4 Add the themes to the captions and then write a publisher's blurb which details the main events of the story and outlines the main themes which appear in it.

Follow-up

- For more on key incidents, see the following unit.
- For more on story, plot, and theme, see pages 86–87.

Key Incidents

Linking Key Incidents to Themes

Read the following extract, in which a boy called Kingshaw is alone in a field of corn.

I'm the King of the Castle

The cornfield was high up. He stood in the very middle of it now, and the sun came glaring down. He could feel the sweat running over his back, and in the creases of his thighs. His face was burning. He sat down, although the stubble pricked at him, through his jeans, and looked over at the dark line of trees on the edge of Hang Wood. They seemed very close – all the individual branches were clearly outlined. The fields around him were absolutely still.

When he first saw the crow, he took no notice. There had been several crows. This one glided down into the corn on its enormous, ragged wings. He began to be aware of it when it rose up suddenly, circled overhead, and then dived, to land not very far away from him. Kingshaw could see the feathers on its head, shining black in between the butter-coloured corn-stalks. Then it rose, and circled, and came down again, this time not quite landing, but flapping about his head, beating its wings and making a sound like flat leather pieces being slapped together. It was the largest crow he had ever seen. As it came down for the third time, he looked up and noticed its beak, opening in a screech. The inside of its mouth was scarlet, it had small glinting eyes.

Kingshaw got up and flapped his arms. For a moment, the bird retreated a little way off, and higher up in the sky. He began to walk rather quickly back, through the path in the corn, looking ahead of him. Stupid to be scared of a rotten bird. What could a bird do? But he felt his own extreme isolation, high up in the cornfield.

For a moment, he could only hear the soft thudding of his own footsteps, and the silky sound of the corn, brushing against him. Then, there was a rush of air, as the great crow came beating down, and wheeled about his head. The beak opened and the hoarse caaw came out again and again, from inside the scarlet mouth.

Kingshaw began to run, not caring now if he trampled the corn, wanting to get away, down into the next field. He thought that the corn might be some kind of crow's food store, in which he was seen as an invader. Perhaps this was only the first of a whole battalion of crows, that would rise up and swoop at him. Get on to the grass then, he thought, get on to the grass, that'll be safe, it'll go away. He wondered if it had mistaken him for some hostile animal, lurking down in the corn.

His progress was very slow, through the cornfield, the thick stalks bunched together and got in his way, and he had to shove them back with his arms. But he reached the gate and climbed it, and dropped on to the grass of the field on the other side. Sweat was running down his forehead and into his eyes. He looked up. The crow kept on coming. He ran.

But it wasn't easy to run down this field, either, because of the tractor ruts. He began to leap wildly from side to side of them, his legs stretched as wide as they could go, and for a short time, it seemed that he did go faster. The crow dived again, and, as it rose, Kingshaw felt the tip of its black wing, beating against his face. He gave a sudden, dry sob. Then, his left foot caught in one of the ruts and he keeled over, going down straight forwards.

Susan Hill

Activity

1 Once you have read the passage, make a chart like the one below to help you identify how themes and key incidents are linked. Pick out key words and phrases paragraph by paragraph.

Paragraph 1	Key Words and Phrases
Key Incident	Kingshaw was alone in a field of corn. It was very hot.
Setting	cornfield high up dark line of trees close Hang Wood fields absolutely still
Kingshaw	sweat running face burning stubble pricked
Crow	

2 Now, taking each paragraph in turn, write a short piece about the themes you have identified. The first paragraph has been done for you.

> From evidence in the first paragraph it seems that Kingshaw is uncomfortable and out of place – even the stubble 'pricked at him'. The crow hasn't appeared yet, but the setting increases the feeling that Kingshaw is out of place here – the cornfield is 'high up' and 'absolutely still', and the frightening 'Hang Wood' is a 'dark line'. It seems as if the author is emphasizing the boy's loneliness and isolation and although Kingshaw isn't actually afraid at this point, the atmosphere is threatening.

Follow-up

- For more help on themes, see pages 86–87 and 110–111.
- For help on quoting from a text, see the following unit.

Quoting From a Text

Objectives:

- to learn how to gather direct evidence from a text
- to learn how to quote such evidence in a piece of writing

Using Quotations

When you are writing in response to texts, you need to be able to show precisely what you have read and understood. To do this effectively you will need to know how to use direct quotation of words and phrases – evidence from the passage – to help you complete the task.

- If you are quoting single words or short phrases, these need to be woven into the flow of your sentence, and marked off with quotation marks. The previous unit gives a good example of this:

  > Kingshaw is out of place here – the cornfield is 'high up' and 'absolutely still', and the frightening 'Hang Wood' is a 'dark line'.

- If you are quoting a much longer piece, or lines from a poem, they should still be marked off with quotation marks and then be set out on a separate line or lines.

The Scarecrows

choice of language	
things that represent danger	

In this book Simon is sure that an old mill is evil. He is determined to destroy it and, here, is running towards it through the night, trying to give himself courage by remembering his father (a soldier killed in the war) and the advice he would have given.

Although written in the third person, the story seems personal. The language all through is like the running commentary of a rugby match.

'Run, Simon, run!'
Run, Simon, run. Like on the rugby-field. All the kids, all the masters shouting, and the ball in his hands.

He ran. Smashed through the hedge as if it were a rugby-pack. Felt the branches clutch at his shirt and tear away despairingly.

Language of movement. Can you find more?

He darted between the figures of the scarecrows. Starkey[1] was still lurking at the back. He almost ran into him, into the filthy smell of rotting straw; but swerved just in time. The turnip-leaves, full of rain, lashed his ankles like whips and threw wet up his trousers. He trampled on the rounded bodies of the turnips as if he was in a black room full of hard solid rugby-balls.

Language of horror and danger. Can you find more?

He is alone but not lonely, as he feels supported by the example of his father.

He didn't run for help to the village. *He* had the ball; nobody else could carry it now. He was alone. Nobody backing-up. This was how it felt to be alone. Not terrible, but marvellous. This was how father must have felt, driving his jeep at the Flossies[2] ... Father hadn't really been lonely. He'd simply been *alone*. He felt at one with his father at last. *Head straight for what you're scared of, Simon. It'll usually run away, if you do. If not, you're no worse off ...* With father there, he no longer cared if he lived or died.

He runs straight towards the danger, determined and desperate to reach his goal.

He was panting now; great gouts of breath. Panting in total darkness, but still running, running for the mill. And somehow he knew, in all that turnip-filled darkness, just exactly where the mill was. If he was tied beyond hope to the mill, the mill was also tied beyond hope to him. It couldn't escape him, no more than he could escape it.

Run straight at your enemy. And, in running, gasping, falling and getting up, he became aware of some kind of power in himself. When he got to the mill, he would know what to do. He knew that; and somehow the mill knew it too. Somehow, he sensed the mill was afraid; and that made his legs strong.

He was running head-down. Something – maybe the end of the turnips – made him look up. Just in time. He teetered on the very brink of the mill-dam. One more step and he would have been into the mill pool, where the sides were too high to climb out, and he would have sunk down through the sooty depths, into the grey scummy arms of the weed.

Exciting narrative detail. Can you find more?

Hard *luck*! He flung the thought at the mill, wolfishly. Turned left and ran along the dam-wall. The smell of the pool came up to his nostrils. But the pool was too late to catch him now.

Down the steps past the mill-race. It gaped at his feet in the dark, waiting for him. It was as if his feet were running on a knife-edge. But he ran true. The door smashed open as he hit it. Splintered more easily that he expected it to.

Here the passage reaches its climax.

Wood splintering ... *smash, smash, smash*.

He ran through the living-room, sending table and chair crashing in the dark.

The language of violence. Can you find any more?

Smash, smash. SMASH. Smash wood.

He fought his way upstairs. Ropes snatched at his face, strong, thick and hairy. He ran to the hanging sack, dangling heavy over its trapdoor. He felt his feet teetering on the sharp stair-edges, over pits of dark.

Robert Westall

Footnotes

[1] the name Simon has given to one of the scarecrows.

[2] the enemy soldiers Simon's father had fought.

Activity

From your close reading of the passage, write down how you think Simon faces up to danger on his own. Highlight parts of the text that you think could act as evidence. For example:

- What is the danger?
- How does he face it? Look at the comparisons with a rugby match, the imagined advice from his father.
- How is he described as being alone?

Comment particularly on how the author's choice of language builds up a sense of excitement. Look at the language of movement, horror, danger, and violence. Weave short quotations into your final written answer.

Follow-up

- For help on identifying major themes, see pages 110–111.
- For help on identifying key incidents, see pages 112–113.
- For help analysing aspects of style, see pages 94–95.

Writing a Book Review

Reading a Book

The more you know about your reading habits, the more you should enjoy reading. Take some time now to think about your reading habits.

- Where do you like to read? In the bath? On a comfy chair? On the floor? In bed?
- Do you like silence? Noise? Music? TV?
- Do you like a lot of time? Just a few minutes?
- How do you choose your books? With a teacher? Friend? Parent? Librarian? By the cover?
- What do you look for? Good story? Problems you can share? New ideas? Surprising endings? Realistic characters?
- What happens when you read? Do you ever laugh? Cry? Become part of the world of the book, imagining people and places in your head? Get bored?
- Do you enjoy TV adaptations of books?

If you do enjoy reading, why do you think this is? If you are not keen on reading, what do you think the reasons for this are?

Keeping a Reading Log

It's a good idea to keep a reading diary or log where you can jot down impressions, thoughts, feelings, or pictures while you are reading. In this way it will be easier to remember which parts of a story you enjoyed or were puzzled about. If you pause and think like this as you read, you will end up understanding a story much better.

Activity

Choose a book that you have just finished reading. Gather your ideas about it in the form of a chart, a series of pictures, or a poster. Your ideas could include the following:

- a description of two or three key incidents in the story
- a description of the main characters – how they look and behave
- a description of the important places – what happens there
- two or three themes and ideas that are important in the story
- two or three different moods in the story

Now turn these ideas into a carefully paragraphed book review. Remember that a book review is usually a personal response to what has been read, so it may not always be a balanced view. You do need to give the person who will be reading your review factual details about the book, but you also need to try and inform them and persuade them to accept your point of view. Try to back up your review with examples and quotations from the text.

What is the book about?

- Give an outline of the key incidents in the story.

Who are the main characters?

- Describe who the characters are in terms of personality and behaviour and the sort of problems they have to face.

Setting and atmosphere?

- When describing the main setting of the story, concentrate on the sort of atmosphere or mood that has been created.

Main themes and ideas?

- What are the main themes and ideas that the author was trying to get you to understand?

Personal response

- How do you feel about the book?
- Try to explain which parts of the story held your interest, made you smile, made you sad or frightened, or made you think.
- Was the ending one that you expected or not?
- What kind of people might enjoy the book?
- Have you learned anything from it about life or life's problems?
- How does it compare with any other similar books you have read?

Follow-up

- For more help on all aspects of responding to a text, see the Reading Literature Section, pages 86–107.

Comparing Prose Texts

- to learn how to draw out similarities and differences between texts and how to develop these ideas in writing

First Impressions

Look carefully at the following book covers and story openings.

Chapter One

When I was a lad, before I met Valerie, nothing ever seemed to die.

My Dad would look up from the local paper sometimes, with a sad or pale face. But he wouldn't say, 'Jack Smith's dead.' He'd say, 'I see poor Jack Smith's gotten away.' And I would have a vision of Jack Smith on the run, like an escaped convict in a movie, maybe in rags, but definitely heading for somewhere better. To that eternal life the vicar went on about endlessly in church, three times every Sunday, perhaps . . .

I only ever saw two dead creatures. On a day out to a lighthouse up the Northumbrian coast, I saw a dead seagull; a pretty little thing, a kittiwake I think. Somebody had made a nest for it, from seaweed on a ledge in the cliff. Its eyes were shut, but every soft feather was in place. I stroked them.

'It just looks asleep,' said my mother.

'It'll get a good rest now,' said my Dad.

The whole place seemed filled with love.

The other dead thing was the ginger cat in Billing's Mill. Billing's Mill dominated our skyline, up on its hill; all its sails gone, a squat empty milk-bottle of blackened stone. A sort of castle keep, in which the tom-cat's body lay, a thing of terror and challenge

1

Chapter One

Sergeant Millom got up on the twenty-seventh of May after another sleepless night. Outside his one-man police station, the sun shone on the little river that danced through the village. The clock in the tall tower of Beaminster church chimed eight, disturbing the pigeons on the parapet. A horse and cart passed, its clop and rumble echoing between the honey-coloured houses.

It should have been peaceful, but the warm east wind carried, like persistent distant thunder, the rumble of German guns. Jerry had reached the French Channel Ports. The King of the Belgians had surrendered. The British Expeditionary Force and their commander, Lord Gort, were trapped around Dunkirk with their backs against the sea.

The news on the radio sickened Sergeant Millom. All the tripe about planned strategic withdrawals, and our troops being in high fighting spirits, and how many Jerry tanks the French 75s were knocking out. The newspapers sickened him, too, with photographs of grinning Tommies giving the thumbs-up. Probably photos a month old. They wouldn't be grinning now, poor sods. Even if they weren't lying dead in some Belgian ditch with the rats at them. Sergeant Millom

1

Activity

1 To compare the material on each of the books on page 118, copy out the chart below and try to fill in as many details as you can. Think about the following as you fill it in:

- **Title** Do they have any words or ideas in common?
- **Cover** Is there a similarity of style, mood, or pictures?
- **Blurb** Are there common settings, problems, characters, or events described?
- **First Page** Do these include speech, description, or a problem? Are there any similarities or major differences?

	The Promise	Blitzcat
Title		
Cover		
Blurb		
First Page		

2 Now write a report of the similarities and differences that you have found so far. Use the information gathered in the chart to help you. How do you expect each story to continue?

Working on

Compare two complete stories that you have read. Either choose two by the same author, or two which explore similar topics. Start with the above guidelines, but continue your chart and research to include the following categories of comparison:

- plot
- main themes
- key incidents
- main characters
- main setting
- mood – how does it develop?
- storyteller – how successful is the narrative voice?
- language – is it striking in any way?

Now write up your ideas. Remember to include examples and quotations.

Follow-up

- For more help on all aspects of responding to texts, see the Reading Literature Section, pages 86–107.

Comparing Poems

The Diary of Dorothy Wordsworth

(March 14th) Sunday Morning. William had slept badly – he got up at nine o'clock, but before he rose he had finished *The Beggar Boys*, and while we were at breakfast that is (for I had breakfasted) he, with his basin of broth before him untouched, and a little plate of bread and butter, wrote the poem *To a Butterfly*! He ate not a morsel, nor put on his stockings, but sat with his shirt neck unbuttoned, and his waist coat open while he did it. The thought first came upon him as we were talking about the pleasure we both always feel at the sight of a butterfly. I told him that I used to chase them a little, but that I was afraid of brushing the dust off their wings, and did not catch them. He told me how they used to kill the white ones when he went to school because they were Frenchmen. Mr Simpson came in just as he was finishing the poem. After he was gone I wrote it down and the other poems, and I read them over to him.

Dorothy Wordsworth

To a Butterfly

Rhythm of 8 syllables per line

Metaphor

Stuctured rhyme scheme

Change of tone

Contrast of characters with change of tone and vocabulary

Alliteration

Stay near me – do not take thy flight!
A little longer stay in sight!
Much converse do I find in thee,
Historian of my infancy!
Float near me; do not yet depart!
Dead times revive in thee:
Thou bring'st, gay creature as thou art!
A solemn image to my heart,
My father's family!
Oh! Pleasant, pleasant were the days,
The time, when, in our childish plays,
My sister Emmeline and I
Together chased the butterfly!
A very hunter did I rush
Upon the prey: – with leaps and springs
I followed on from brake to bush;
But she, God love her, feared to brush
The dust from off its wings.

William Wordsworth

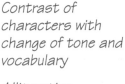

Activity

1   Read the diary extract and the poem *To a Butterfly* carefully and try to find:
- what ideas William Wordsworth has used from his conversation with Dorothy
- what he adds to make it more than a memory of when they were children

2 What sort of person do you think the narrator of *To a Butterfly* is? Does reading Dorothy's diary help us to understand any details more clearly?

Was Worm

Was worm

swaddled in white
Now tiny queen
in sequin coat
peacockbright

drinks the wind
and feeds
on sweat of the leaves

Is little chinks
of mosaic floating
a scatter
of coloured beads

Alighting pokes
with her new black wire
the saffron yokes

On silent hinges
openfolds her wings'
applauding hands
Weaned

from coddling white
to lakedeep air
to blue and green

Is queen

May Swenson

Working on

1 Read the poems *To a Butterfly* and *Was Worm* carefully and copy them out. Then make notes on your copies. Highlight any literary techniques, and also any words, phrases, or images that please or puzzle you. Some notes have been added to *To a Butterfly* to help you begin.

2 Copy out the chart below and try to fill in as many details as you can. Think about the following as you fill it in:
   • subject – what are the poems about?
   • style – how have they been written? (look at layout, punctuation, sentence-structure, rhyme, rhythm, choice of words)
   • tone – is the tone calm? strange? excited? observant?
   • similarities – can you detect any common features between the poems?
   • differences – what differences can you find? (look at form, shape, tense, imagery, tone)

	To a Butterfly	Was Worm
Subject		
Style		
Tone		
Similarities		
Differences		

Using all the ideas you have gathered, write a detailed comparison of the two poems. Also explain which poem you prefer and why.

Follow-up

• For more help on analysing poetry, see pages 98–101.

Writing About Shakespeare

Objectives:

- to develop a written response to a scene from Shakespeare, focusing on character, language, and dramatization, and supporting the response with textual reference

A Scene from *Henry IV*

The extract below comes from Shakespeare's play *Henry IV*. In a battle for King Henry, Hotspur had taken some prisoners but later refused to hand them over to a lord who had arrived on the battlefield fashionably dressed and smelling of sweet perfumes. Hotspur, faint and exhausted from the fighting, was extremely annoyed by this man. In this scene Hotspur is having to explain his annoyance at the court of King Henry.

Henry IV

Act 1, Scene 3

Hotspur: My <u>liege</u>[1], I did deny no prisoners,
But I remember when the fight was done,
When I was dry with rage and extreme toil,
Breathless and faint, leaning upon my sword,
Came there a certain lord, neat, and trimly dress'd,
Fresh as a bridegroom, and his chin new reap'd
Show'd like a stubble-land at harvest-home;
He was perfumed like a milliner,
And 'twixt his finger and his thumb he held
A <u>pouncet-box</u>[2], which ever and anon
He gave his nose and took't away again;
Who therewith angry, when it next came there,
Took it in snuff – and still he smil'd and talk'd –
And as the soldiers bore dead bodies by,
He call'd them untaught knaves, unmannerly,
To bring a slovenly unhandsome <u>corse</u>[3]
Betwixt the wind and his nobility.
With many <u>holiday and lady terms</u>[4]
He questioned me: amongst the rest, demanded
My prisoners in your Majesty's behalf.
I then, all smarting with my wounds being cold,
To be so pest'red with a <u>popinjay</u>[5],
Out of my grief and my impatience

Answer'd neglectingly I know not what –
He should, or he should not – for he made me mad
To see him shine so brisk, and smell so sweet,
And talk so like a waiting-gentlewoman
Of guns, and drums, and wounds – God save the mark! –
And telling me the sovereignest thing[6] on earth
Was parmaceti[7] for an inward bruise;
And that it was great pity, so it was,
This villainous saltpetre[8] should be digg'd
Out of the bowels of the harmless earth,
Which many a good tall fellow had destroy'd
So cowardly; and but for these vile guns
He would himself have been a soldier.
This bald unjointed chat of his, my lord,
I answered indirectly, as I said;
And I beseech you, let not his report
Come current[9] for an accusation
Betwixt my love and your high Majesty.

William Shakespeare

Footnotes

[1] lord   [2] a small box for perfumes
[3] corpse   [4] dainty and feminine expressions
[5] parrot   [6] the best remedy
[7] a medical preparation used like a cream
[8] used in making gunpowder   [9] be considered true

In Hotspur's speech we have a good example of how Shakespeare can describe characters and situations in vivid concrete language.

Activity

1 Make notes on the following questions – quote all the information you can find and explain what you think the meanings are in your own words.
   • What is Hotspur like?
   • What is the 'certain lord' like? Make sure you include and explain the main phrases that Hotspur uses to describe him.
   • What details or information can you find about the battle?
   • Find some examples of how Hotspur's language is quite down-to-earth when he is expressing his own feelings.
   • If you were the director of the play, where would you tell Hotspur to mimic and make fun of the speech and actions of the lord? (Quote the lines.)

2 Now write a comparison between the character and behaviour of Hotspur and that of the lord. Add what your opinion is of them both. Make sure you quote some evidence from the text.

Follow-up

• For more help on reading Shakespeare, see pages 102–103.
• For help on analysing characters, see pages 108–109.

Assignment: Comparing Genres 2

The Ice Dragons

They tell of Polar dragons
Who breathe frost instead of fire,
With icicles nine along their backs,
Each one a glassy spire.
In the eerie light
Of that endless white
Where bleak winds always blow,
They make their homes
Neath icy domes
In everlasting snow.
And when these dragons gather
(This is the tale that's told)
They stand in an Arctic Circle,
They breathe,
And the world grows cold.

Eric Finney

A Sound of Thunder

It came on great oiled, resilient, striding legs. It towered thirty
feet above half of the trees, a great evil god, folding its delicate
watchmaker's claws close to its oily reptilian chest. Each lower leg was
a piston, a thousand pounds of white bone, sunk in thick ropes of
muscle, sheathed over in a gleam of pebbled skin like the mail of a
terrible warrior. Each thigh was a ton of meat, ivory, and steel mesh.
And from the great breathing cage of the upper body those two
delicate arms dangled out in front, arms with hands which might
pick up and examine men like toys, while the snake neck coiled …
Its mouth gaped, exposing a fence of teeth like daggers. Its eyes rolled,
ostrich eggs, empty of all expression, save hunger …

The Monster, at the first motion, lunged forward with a terrible
scream. It covered one hundred yards in four seconds. The rifles
jerked up and blazed fire. A windstorm from the beast's mouth
engulfed them in the stench of slime and old blood. The Monster
roared, teeth glittering with sun …

The rifles cracked again. Their sound was lost in shriek and lizard
thunder. The great lever of the reptile's tail swung up, lashed sideways.
Trees exploded in clouds of leaf and branch. The Monster twitched its
jeweller's hands down to fondle the men, to twist them in half, to crush
them like berries, to cram them into its teeth and its screaming throat.

Its boulder-stone eyes levelled with the men. They saw themselves mirrored. They fired at the metallic eyelids and the blazing black iris.

Like a stone idol, like a mountain avalanche, Tyrannosaurus fell. Thundering, it clutched trees, pulled them with it. It wrenched and tore the metal path. The men flung themselves back and away. The body hit, ten tons of cold flesh and stone. The guns fired. The Monster lashed its armoured tail, twitched its snake jaws, and lay still. A fount of blood spurted from its throat. Somewhere inside, a sac of fluids burst. Sickening gushes drenched the hunters. They stood, red and glistening.

The thunder faded.

Ray Bradbury

The Tempest

Trinculo: What have we here? A man or a fish? Dead or alive? A fish: he smells like a fish; a very ancient and fish-like smell; a kind of not of the newest Poor-John. A strange fish! Were I in England now – as once I was – and had but this fish painted, not a holiday fool there but would give a piece of silver: there would this monster make a man; any strange beast there makes a man … Legg'd like a man! And his fins like arms! Warm, o' my troth! I do now let loose my opinion, hold it no longer; this is no fish, but an islander, that hath lately suffered by a thunderbolt.

Trinculo creeps under the monster Caliban's cloak to shelter from a storm. His legs and Caliban's stick out at opposite ends. Stephano, Trinculo's friend, now comes in. As usual, he is clutching a bottle and is drunk. He accidentally kicks the covered shapes of Caliban and Trinculo.

Stephano: Four legs and two voices; a most delicate monster! His forward voice now is to speak well of his friend; his backward voice is to utter foul speeches and to detract. If all the wine in my bottle will recover him, I will help his ague. Come. Amen! I will pour some in thy other mouth.

William Shakespeare

Activity   Compare each of the monsters described – it might help to draw them, concentrating on the different details of their appearance.
- How are we meant to feel about them – what evidence can you find? Quote single words and short phrases within the flow of your writing.
- What can you tell from the language used to describe them? Are there many words of action, of horror, of humour?
- Which description do you find the most effective? Why do you think this is?
- Does the form of the writing (poem, story, play) have any bearing on the final effect that the monster has? Why do you think this is?

Follow-up   • For help on this assignment, see the Reading Literature Section, pages 86–107.

Glossary

accent the way words are pronounced. This usually depends on where someone lives and who they mix with.

adjective a describing word, giving more information about a noun or pronoun: e.g. My desk is *old* and *wobbly* and very *dirty*!

adverb adverbs give more information about verbs, adjectives, or other adverbs: e.g. She asked me *nicely*.

alliteration repeating the same initial letter of a word: e.g. **S**ean **s**lipped unobtrusively into school.

apostrophe a punctuation mark used to show:

- that letters have been missed out: e.g. I can't (can *no*t) do that.
- ownership/possession: e.g. The dog's tail (tail *of the dog*) was wagging.

assonance the repeating of vowel sounds in the middle of words: e.g. 'The w*ee*ping willow sw*ee*ps its l*ea*ves across the grass.'

authorial voice the style an author chooses in writing a story.

- **first person** writing from the point of view of a particular character using 'I': e.g. I love this.
- **third person** writing more objectively as an outsider looking on, using 'he', 'she', 'they' or 'it': e.g. He loved the new bike.

autobiography the story of your own life.

biography the story of someone else's life.

blurb the piece of writing on a book cover that gives a short description of what the book is about.

clause a group of words which forms part of a sentence and has a subject and predicate of its own.

cliché an idea or a phrase that is used too often.

comma , a punctuation mark which is used to break up and separate parts of a sentence.

colon : a punctuation mark which is used to introduce a list, statement, or saying.

conjunction a word which is used to join other words together: e.g. and, but, or.

demonstrative pronoun a word which shows what is being referred to: e.g. this, that, these, those.

dialect form of speech which includes differences in words, grammar, and accent, showing which country or part of a country people come from.

diction a way of using words.

direct speech spoken words reproduced in writing, e.g. 'Can I go?' he asked.

exclamation mark ! a punctuation mark used at the end of a sentence to show shock or surprise.

full stop . a punctuation mark used to show the end of a sentence or shortened forms of words.

genre writing in a particular form, e.g. Romance, Horror, Science Fiction.

grammar the way words are arranged in sentences, and the study of this, according to established rules.

imagery in description, the use of comparison in order to make something more vivid. (See 'simile', 'metaphor', 'personification'.)

internal rhyme in poetry, where rhymes occur in the middle of a line rather than at the end.

inverted commas the punctuation marks which are used to show speech.

irony in speech, saying the opposite of what you really mean. In writing, there is the sense of a shared secret between those who know the real meaning of the words, against those who are unaware of it.

metaphor a way of comparing two things, where the comparison is not made obvious: 'You are a pig!' (See 'simile')

narrative writing or speaking which tells a story.

noun the word in a sentence which names people, places, things, or ideas.

- **abstract noun** the name given to something you cannot touch, such as a feeling, an emotion, or an idea: e.g. hunger, love.

- **collective noun** the name given to groups of people, animals, or things: e.g. a *bunch* of flowers.

- **common noun** a name given to people, animals, or things: e.g. baby, flower, cat.

- **proper noun** the name of a particular person, place, or thing: e.g. Ann, London, Fido.

onomatopoeia where the sound of something is linked to its name: e.g. bang, crash, ping.

paragraph a way of organizing sentences into linked blocks.

personification a form of metaphor, where an object or idea is described as if it were a person.

phrase a group of words that makes sense but is incomplete. (See 'sentence')

plot the main events in a story and how they are linked together.

plural the form of a noun or verb when it stands for more than one person or thing. (See 'singular')

prefix a group of letters that comes at the beginning of a word. (See 'suffix')

preposition a word that is always followed by a noun or pronoun which together tell where or how something happens: e.g. on, near, after.

pronoun a word used in place of a noun: e.g. he, she.

pronunciation the way words are spoken or pronounced.

prose writing, in sentences – different from verse and notes.

question mark ? a punctuation mark which is used to show a question has been asked.

Received Pronunciation the accent which does not belong to a particular place and which is used by a large number of educated and influential people.

reported speech the report of what somebody has said rather than the actual words spoken.

rhetoric and **rhetorical devices** using words impressively, because they sound good.

rhetorical question a question that is asked when an answer isn't expected: e.g. 'I wonder how many of you eat a proper breakfast?'

rhyme when two or more words have the same or similar sounds.

rule of three using three different examples for emphasis in speech or writing: e.g. 'Young people today are loyal, thoughtful, and hardworking.'

semi-colon ; a punctuation mark that shows a stronger pause than a comma, but a weaker pause than a full stop.

sentence a group of words, beginning with a capital letter and ending with a full stop, question mark, or exclamation mark which makes sense on their own. (See 'phrase')

simile a way of comparing two things using the words *like* or *as* where the comparison is obvious: e.g.'You eat like a pig!' or 'You are as greedy as a pig!'

singular the form of a noun or verb when it stands for only one person or thing. (See 'plural')

slang an informal or casual use of language that is a private way of talking between particular groups of people.

Standard English the form of language used for almost all types of formal communication in all parts of Britain.

suffix a group of letters added to the end of a word. (See 'prefix')

synonym a word which has the same or similar meaning to another word.

tense the form of a verb which shows when something is happening – past, present, or future.

transcript the written version of the actual words someone has spoken.

verb 'doing' word: e.g. 'He *is* there' or 'She *runs* home'. Verbs make sentences work and give information about what is happening.

verse the single line of a poem or a division in a poem, similar to a paragraph in prose.

vocabulary the range and choice of words available in language.

word class the category to which a word belongs depending on the way it is used in a sentence: e.g. noun, verb, adjective, adverb, etc.

Wider Reading List

Fiction

Robert Westall, *The Scarecrows*
(Chatto and Windus, 1981)

Nina Bawden, *Carrie's War*
(Victor Gollancz, 1973)

Michelle Magorian, *Goodnight Mr Tom*
(Penguin, 1981)

Philippa Pearce, *Tom's Midnight Garden*
(OUP, 1958)

Nigel Hinton, *Buddy*
(J M Dent and Sons, 1982)

Berlie Doherty, *Granny Was A Buffer Girl*
(Armada, 1988)

George Orwell, *Animal Farm*
(Martin, Secker and Warburg, 1945)

Rukshana Smith, *Sumitra's Story*
(The Bodley Head Children's Books 1982)

Charles Dickens, *A Christmas Carol*
(Penguin, 1984)

Poetry

Selected by Michael Rosen, *The Kingfisher Book
of Children's Poetry* (Kingfisher Books, 1985)

Merrick and Fox, *Poems From Other Ages*
(Collins Educational, 1983)

David Kitchen ed., *Axed between the Ears* (Heinemann,
1987)

The Oxford Book of Story Poems, Harrison and Stuart-
Clark (OUP, 1990)

Hughes and Heaney ed., *Rattlebag* (Faber, 1982)

Michael and Peter Benton ed., *Touchstones 1–3*
(Hodder & Stoughton, 1987–1988))

Roger McGough ed., *Strictly Private* (Penguin, 1988)

The Oxford Treasury of Children's Poems (OUP, 1988)

Drama

Anne Fine, *The Granny Project*
(Collins Educational, 1986)

Dylan Thomas, *Under Milkwood*
(Everyman, 1995)

Gene Kemp, *The Turbulent Term of Tyke Tiler*
(OUP, 1990)

Mary Shelley – adapted by Philip Pullman,
Frankenstein (OUP, 1990)

Marjorie Darke – adapted by Lucas & Keaney,
A Question of Courage (OUP, 1990)

Nigel Gray – adapted by Ann Cheetham,
Black Harvest (Collins Educational, 1986)

Helen Forrester – adapted by Valerie Windsor,
Twopence to Cross the Mersey
(Collins, 1987)

Joan Lingard – adapted by David Neville, *Across the
Barricades* (OUP, 1990)

Non-Fiction

Maureen Dunbar, *Catherine* (Viking, 1986)

Zlata Filipovic, *Zlata's Diary* (Viking, 1994)

Anne Frank, *The Diary of Anne Frank*
(Vallentine Mitchell and Co, 1953)

Gerald Durrell, *My Family and Other Animals*
(Rupert Hart-Davis, 1956)

Felix Pryor ed., *The Faber Book of Letters* (Faber, 1990)

Ronald Blythe ed, *The Penguin Book of Diaries*
(Penguin, 1991)

Bob Geldof, *Is That It?* (Penguin, 1986)

Jonathan Raban, *The Oxford Book of the Sea*,
(OUP, 1982)

Bernadette Vallely, *The Young Person's Guide to Saving
the Planet* (Virago, 1990)

Freya Stark, *A Winter in Arabia*
(John Murray, 1940)

English Language

Bill Bryson, *Mother Tongue* (Penguin, 1991)

David Crystal, *English Language* (Penguin, 1990)

Betty Rosen, *And None of it was Nonsense*
(Mary Glasgow, 1988)

OXFORD
UNIVERSITY PRESS

Great Clarendon Street, Oxford OX2 6DP

Oxford New York

Athens Auckland Bangkok Bogotá Buenos Aires Calcutta Cape Town
Chennai Dar es Salaam Delhi Florence Hong Kong Istanbul Karachi
Kuala Lumpur Madrid Melbourne Mexico City Mumbai Nairobi
Paris São Paulo Singapore Taipei Tokyo Toronto Warsaw

and associated companies in Berlin Ibadan

Oxford is a registered trade mark of Oxford University Press
in the UK and certain other countries

© Liz Lockwood 1996

The moral rights of the author have been asserted
Database right Oxford University Press (maker)

First published 1996
Reprinted 1997, 1998 (twice), 2000

ISBN 0 19 831290 3

Printed in Spain